FOOD POLICY REVIEW 1

Institutional Finance
for Agricultural Development
An Analytical Survey of Critical Issues

BHUPAT M. DESAI

JOHN W. MELLOR

INTERNATIONAL FOOD POLICY RESEARCH INSTITUTE
WASHINGTON, D.C.

Library of Congress Cataloging-
in-Publication Data

Desai, B. M. (Bhupat Maganlal), 1938-
   Institutional finance for agricultural development : an analytical survey of critical issues /
Bhupat M. Desai and John W. Mellor.
      p.   cm. — (Literature review series : 1)
   Includes bibliographical references.
   ISBN 0-89629-500-1
   1. Agricultural credit—Developing countries.
2. Agricultural credit corporations—Developing
countries. 3. Rural credit—Developing countries.
4. Interest rates—Developing countries. I. Mellor,
John Williams, 1928-   . II. Title. III. Series.

HG2051.D44D47 1993   93-34703
332.7'1'091724—dc20   CIP

Contents

Tables

Illustrations

Foreword

This report introduces a new series of IFPRI publications called Food Policy Review. As IFPRI moves into new fields of inquiry in implementing its research plan for the next five years, we feel the need for substantive syntheses of the findings presented in the literature on major issues and topics. These rigorously juried works are expected to be far more than scholarly literature reviews. They are likely to include original research on possible policy options available to developing-country policymakers, based on the results presented in the current literature, and to help point the way to further research needs.

The role of access to rural credit facilities in food security has been an area of increasing concern at IFPRI. Institutions such as the Grameen Bank in India (see Research Report 65) enhance the ability of the poor to purchase food during seasonal shortfalls, promote the use of new technologies, and contribute to capital investment and education opportunities. Food Policy Review 1, by Bhupat M. Desai and John W. Mellor, examines the large body of literature on rural financial institutions in both developing and developed countries to determine how such institutions are best organized, how they can improve their financial viability, and how real interest rates affect the demand for rural loans, the supply of deposits, and savings. It is an excellent work to initiate what is expected to be a valuable new publications series.

Per Pinstrup-Andersen
Director General

Acknowledgments

We are particularly grateful for the generous help of Dale W. Adams, without which this study would not have been possible. He facilitated our access to the valuable library collection at Ohio State University, guided us to the voluminous literature generated by the program with which he has long been associated, constructively commented on the initial research proposal and notes, and argued long and hard with us on points of disagreement. Some such disagreement continues, even though muted as a result of our discussions, and provides a basis for further research. We are also grateful to Carlos E. Cuevas, Douglas H. Graham, and Richard L. Meyer, also of Ohio State University, for sharing their pioneering work and for encouraging discussion.

We are equally grateful to the members and others associated with the Reserve Bank of India's Agricultural Credit Committee, on which John Mellor served, and particularly to the chairman, Ali Khusro; the member secretary, C. V. Nair; and the then governor of the Reserve Bank of India, R. N. Malhotra. Much that is reflected in this report arises from the insights from that major in-depth analysis and from interaction with the various members and associates of the committee.

We are thankful to Raisuddin Ahmed, Harold Alderman, Mark Rosegrant, and Stephen Vosti of IFPRI, who commented on the initial proposal and notes. In the course of this study, we received valuable comments from Raisuddin Ahmed, Joachim von Braun, M. L. Dantwala, Gunvant Desai, Hannan Ezekiel, Nurul Islam, Sohail Malik, Michael Lipton, Ajay Oza, Mark Rosegrant, and Vijay S. Vyas. We also thank anonymous reviewers for their comments. Vasant Gandhi, Neville Edirisinghe, Dayanatha Jha, Nabil Khaldi, Shubh Kumar, Bruce Stone, and Sudhir Wanmali made specific contributions at points in the course of the study for which we owe special thanks. We also wish to thank Mark Philipps and Ellen Tipper, whose assistance in literature review and data collation and processing was invaluable, and Sumiter Broca, Rajul Pandya-Lorch, and Suman Rustagi for their timely and competent assistance.

We also had the benefits of comments of the participants of the seminar on technology policy held in early July 1990 at the Hague, where a brief paper on this study was presented. We would especially thank Bruce Tolentino for his comments on that paper.

Finally, we are grateful to the Indian Institute of Management, Ahmedabad, India, for their role in facilitating this research and allowing Bhupat Desai to take the extended leave without which this study could not have been completed.

Bhupat M. Desai
John W. Mellor

1

Summary

This study analyzes two areas of agricultural credit policy: institutional development and interest rates. In the first area, it deals with relative roles of institutional and noninstitutional lenders in the process of economic development; organizational principles for developing rural financial institutions (RFIs); and institutional lenders' transaction (administrative) costs, their economies of scale, and their effects on development. (These economies of scale arise from the volume and composition of business operations.) In the second area, it concentrates on the impact of real interest rates on demand for rural loans, supply of rural financial deposits, and supply of rural savings. The analysis is based on an intensive review of the voluminous literature on rural credit. The range of experience with RFIs is immense, and that experience covers a wide range of conditions. It is high time that such experience was ordered and analyzed for the broad benefit of developing countries. On several issues, it has been possible to use existing data sets to pursue analysis beyond that contained in the published and unpublished sources. Of course, the number of variables relating to rural financial markets is greater than even the large number of studies perused; hence only limited use of standard statistical techniques is made for analyzing relationships. This study depends instead on simple tabulations, leavened in some relatively simple circumstances by regression analysis. Further, extensive use is made of a small number of in-depth case studies to bring out particularly important and complex relationships. Although the studies used vary in quality and in detail, the number of studies is sufficiently large to draw clear conclusions about the central tendency. Such an intensive, systematic, and analytic review of a large literature would be incomplete, if not senseless, if the insights generated along the way were not used to reach clear policy recommendations. Hence, the approach is framed in a manner that points to specific key areas of policy conclusion. This also serves the purpose of sharpening the debate.

In this context, six groups of questions are addressed: (1) Why promote formal RFIs, and what is the historical experience in this regard? (2) What organizational principles are needed to encourage appropriate RFIs? Do such institutions exist, or are they emerging? (3) What are the transaction costs of the RFIs? Are the RFIs viable and sustainable, and why? (4) What is the impact of real interest rates and nonprice factors on rural loan demand, supply of rural deposits, and supply of rural savings? (5) What determines whether an institutional rural financial system is a net contribution to or a drain on public resources? And, (6) what policy conclusions can be drawn from this analysis? In analyzing these questions, two types of nonprice factors are considered: those that relate to the various organizational means for promoting RFIs (for example, the density of coverage of RFIs), and those that relate to the external environment of agriculture and its economic unit, such as technology.

These six issues are pursued because of the limited analysis on the first two questions, inappropriate study of the third question, and inadequate research on the last two questions in the literature reviewed. Errors of omission and commission have led to questionable recommendations and formulation of underlying premises for those recommendations. These include an understated need for public policy to focus on institutional means of fostering growth of RFIs and integrated rural capital markets; premature emphasis on privatization of these institutions; overstatement of the level of and increases in transaction costs, with a consequent, unwarranted conclusion that RFIs are not viable; and assumption of an excessively inelastic response of rural loan demand to the real interest rate and a positive and highly elastic response of supply of rural savings and deposits to real interest rates, with a consequent overemphasis on increase in interest rates as a policy instrument for RFIs.

Much of the above follows from a "demand-following" instead of a "supply-leading" approach to rural finance policy. Based on the premise that this distinction between demand-following and supply-leading finance is artificial and incorrect, in this study particular attention is given to the simultaneity of demand for and supply of finance. Specifically, new technology and increased finance are seen as complementary.

This study shows that in both developed and developing countries formal rural lenders and integrated rural financial markets emerge through a deliberate public policy rather than unguided market forces. This is in substantial part because the financial market transactions, which deal in future events, are innately imperfect. One consequence of public policy is the secular decline in the relative importance of private informal lenders in the process of economic development. In countries like Japan, the Republic of Korea, Taiwan, and the United States (referred to throughout this analysis as countries successful in development of RFIs), publicly supported RFIs have successfully developed, and such institutions are emerging in an increasing number of developing countries, such as Bangladesh, Egypt, India, Malaysia, Syria, and Thailand. Although often prompted by financial crises, financial restructuring has in recent years taken forms that have led to lower savings rates, higher inflation rates, lower economic growth, and bankruptcy of the financial institutions. Examples are drawn from Argentina, Brazil, Chile, Turkey, and Uruguay. The unfavorable results arose from the decline in loanable funds, perhaps due to elimination of public institutions, with inadequate attention to the alternatives available, reduced substitution of financial deposits for unproductive forms of saving, high substitutability of financial deposits for productive capital formation, and high interest rates that encourage indiscriminate lending. Thus, restructuring RFIs proves to be a complex question requiring careful analysis and circumspect decisions.

Six organizational principles for developing appropriate RFIs are proposed in this study: (1) promoting multiple RFIs—that is, more than one RFI for a given service area; (2) encouraging a variety of forms of organization of these institutions; (3) ensuring vertical organization of the structure of RFIs from local to regional and national levels; (4) encouraging high geographic density of the field-level offices of RFIs; (5) ensuring that a high proportion of rural clients are reached by them; and (6) promoting diversified and multiple functions that horizontally integrate the agricultural production, input distribution, and marketing and processing subsystems for the benefit of their clients and themselves. The first two of these six principles are the most commonly implemented the world over, including the four successful countries. In almost all countries, multiple instead of single RFIs and a wide variety of forms of organization are found. These include government-supported autonomous public-sector banks and corporations, cooperatives, private commercial banks, and government departments. But many developing countries have RFI systems that are not characterized by the desirable attributes implied by the remaining four organizing principles.

The systems in the four successful countries are both vertically and functionally integrated, with broad, dense coverage of rural areas and population. This has enabled the systems to better realize their basic objectives of rural growth with equity, integration of rural financial markets, and economies of scale and scope (more types of services and larger numbers of them). The rural financial system is generally better organized in Asia than in Sub-Saharan Africa, Latin America and the Caribbean, or the Near East and Mediterranean Basin.

The analysis confirms that the average transaction costs of RFIs are lower when they are vertically integrated, have high geographic density, reach a high proportion of rural clients, and have multiproduct operations that are horizontally integrated. Future policy should accord high priority to improving the last four of the six organizational principles for promoting appropriate RFIs.

The level of interest rates is complex but important to achieving the basic goals of agricultural credit policy. There are two findings, with interacting implications, that are particularly important. First, in developing countries, unlike developed countries, demand for rural loans is elastic with regard to the real interest rate, while the supply of rural deposits and rural savings in general are inelastic. The former arises because interest costs form a significant share in total costs of production when agriculture changes from a subsistence orientation to a market one. But the latter occurs because farmers, being producers, have a lower preference for savings in financial assets than for physical, productive assets. Thus, raising lending and deposit rates has a greater effect in reducing productive investment than in raising deposits, and it has a net effect of reducing the extent to which economies of scale are achieved, with a consequent rise in transaction costs. Of course, interest rates must, over the long run, cover transaction costs as well as the cost of funds. Hence, the levels of deposit rates and transaction costs are important to the level of interest rates. But, due to the relation between interest rates, scale of operation, and transaction costs, there is a causal effect of interest rates on transaction costs and vice versa. The level of real interest rates is a complex issue with vital effects on private investment for agricultural development and on the viability (profitability) of RFIs.

Second, in developing countries, rural borrowing, savings, and deposits are all influenced more by accessibility, liquidity, and safety of these services and availability of related nonfinancial services of RFIs than by interest rates. High density of these institutions is thus critical to the rapid development of larger coverage of geographical areas and rural clients. The effort to realize these benefits initially poses a problem of diseconomies of scale in transaction costs, as well as high administrative costs and loss of discipline associated with rapid expansion. Reducing transaction costs by performing many functions and providing a high density of service would enable RFIs to reduce costs through larger economies of scale and scope rather than through higher interest rates. These are important and complex relations.

Successful examples of such emerging RFIs are the Grameen Bank and the Sonali Bank in Bangladesh; cooperatives, nationalized commercial banks, and to some extent regional rural banks in India; the Bank for Agriculture and Agricultural Cooperatives and lower-level cooperatives in Thailand; two branches of the Agricultural Bank of Sudan in Sudan; and county and township cooperatives in the Republic of Korea. Most of these RFIs have greatly facilitated agricultural development and reaped economies of scale in their transaction costs. They are also viable in that they earn profits and have lower loan delinquency rates. They represent a transition to systems organized around the last four of the earlier-mentioned six organizing principles with their interacting influences.

2

Introduction

Finance and Economic Development

Much of early monetary theory suggests that financial policies affect not only prices, but also output and employment—the real factors in economic development (see Gurley and Shaw 1955, 1960; Keynes 1936; Schumpeter 1934, 1939; Tobin 1965).[1] Similar conclusions are reached through more recent macro finance theories (McKinnon 1973, 1988; Shaw 1973). That causal relation between finance and growth sets the focus for this study, in which the emphasis is on the requisites for development of rural financial policies that facilitate rural growth.

The Keynesians studied the role of money and finance in the context of the Great Depression and occurrence of business cycles. The neo-Keynesians and development economists extended the analysis to issues of economic development (Lewis 1954). This also holds for recent research by Shaw (1973), McKinnon (1973), and their followers, as well as that of their critics (Taylor 1979; van Wijnbergen 1985).

But there is a fundamental difference between the earlier and the more recent literature[2] on finance theories in their recommendations for monetary and financial policies for economic development. For developing countries, the earlier literature considered moderately expansionary but regulated monetary and financial policy to be conducive to encouraging higher and more stable economic growth and employment (Goldsmith 1969; Gurley and Shaw 1955; Keynes 1936; and Taylor 1979). That literature specifically advocated expansion of the institu-

---

[1]The references cited are only examples from a vast literature. To cite them all would be impossible. See, for example, David and Meyer (1983) for evidence on the positive contribution of rural finance policy to farm production and employment.

[2]Earlier literature is represented largely by Keynesians, neo-Keynesians, and development economists, including the major critics of McKinnon and Shaw (Taylor 1979; Tobin 1965; United Nations Secretariat 1980; and van Wijnbergen 1983d to cite a few). Recent literature is largely represented by McKinnon (1973) and Shaw (1973), and their followers (Adams 1977, 1980; Fry 1980, 1988; Gonzalez-Vega 1976; and Von Pischke 1983).

5

tional finance service sector, enactment of usury laws, moderate reserve requirements, ceilings on interest rates, relatively low deposit rates, comparatively low lending rates, and credit allocation targets for socially desirable projects and sectors.

The corresponding policy recommendation from the more recent finance theories is for financial liberalization that relies on market forces. It particularly advocates privatization of financial institutions (including participation by moneylenders), lower reserve requirements, removal of usury laws, elimination of ceilings on interest rates and indexing interest rates to inflation rates, raising deposit and lending rates, and removal of credit quotas (McKinnon 1973; Shaw 1973). But this advocacy has been questioned (De Macedo 1988; Taylor 1979, 1981, 1983; Tobin 1965; and van Wijnbergen 1983a, 1983c, 1983d). The following criticisms can be summarized from the literature that questions liberalization, with examples from such countries as Argentina, Brazil, Chile, the Republic of Korea, Turkey, and Uruguay.

First, such macro changes may lead to cost-push inflation—not only in an arithmetic sense, but also through a process of decline in the supply of loanable funds, due to loss of public lending institutions combined with inadequate rise of private institutions and inadequate substitution of financial deposits for other forms of saving, with a consequent restraint to growth in output.

Second, the argument that the higher interest rates on time deposits will cause higher medium-term growth and a lower inflation rate in the short run is valid only if the shift into time deposits comes out of unproductive assets like cash and commodity stock. But, if this shift is out of productive capital and loans in the informal market, then raising deposit rates can have a negative impact on growth and lead to more— rather than less—inflation.

Third, proposed financial liberalization can also lead to hikes in lending rates, which may encourage indiscriminate lending without proper assessment of the risk of repayment of the credit projects. This leads to an adverse effect on the viability and efficiency of financial institutions, which then may become bankrupt, as well as higher inflation and lower saving and output growth rates.

Fourth, market forces of the neoclassical economic world are notably absent in financial markets. This is because financial markets by definition are imperfect, dealing as they do in future transactions. Moreover, externalities such as weather are particularly important in financial markets.

If these criticisms are extrapolated to rural financial markets and made explicit to rural modernization, a potential can be noted for rural financial institutions (RFIs) to face risks and uncertainties that they resist on their own. But, unless RFIs extend credit to encourage private investment in modern fixed and working capital, agriculture's requirements for new biological and other natural resources for shifting its production function upward cannot be fulfilled. Consequently, the case is built for deliberate promotion of financial institutions by the government, as well as administered interest rates, ceilings on interest rates, and credit quotas (De Macedo 1988; Taylor 1983; Tobin 1965; and van Wijnbergen 1985).

An obvious problem innate to an active government role in development of RFIs is the massive aggregate financial need in the context of very small, fragmented financial markets. That economic problem interacts with the political problem of a populist tradition of repugnance for discipline in lending and repayment, fanned by political interests in using financial markets as a major means of distribution of political patronage—an objective clearly in conflict with economic considerations and the use of the credit system to instill commercial discipline, quite aside from the innate need for financial discipline if the financial system is to remain viable. It is difficult to separate the anecdotal from central tendencies, but there is certainly an impression of widespread corruption, indiscipline, and financial mismanagement in the developing-country financial systems. Later chapters will show that much of this impression is based on misleading accounting systems and lack of understanding of scale economies and the time required to realize them in dispersed rural markets. Even that residual problem is potentially too large to be ignored.

It is nevertheless this concern for bringing discipline to rural financial markets interacting with an orientation to market mechanisms that has brought to analysis of rural financial markets much of what was just discussed as a general financial market point of view. Thus, one can argue that critics take these positions because past agricultural credit policy has neither facilitated agricultural development nor enabled rural financial institutions to be viable (Adams 1977, 1980; Adams and Kato 1978; and Adams, Graham, and Von Pischke 1984). They then recommend much of what has been criticized above (Adams 1977; Gonzalez-Vega 1986). Thus, real interest rates in developing countries are seen as typically low and leading to reduced saving and hence investment rates, inefficient use of credit, unequal distribution of income, and endangered financial viability of institutional lenders. These rates in the critics' judgment are too low, have not reflected the true scarcity of capital, are lower than in informal markets, and have not covered the costs associated with the administration of credit; hence, they have adversely affected the quality of services of institutions. These critics suggest raising nominal interest rates, freely indexing them with the inflation rate, and determining these rates by free operation of market forces. These analyses also, in effect, take a demand-following approach to financial development, which will be discussed later in the context of brief presentations on each of four broad approaches to the role of financial markets in development.

In the early history of the United States, in much of populist literature and perception worldwide, and in many socialist works, the role of finance, especially rural finance, has been perceived to be negative and inconsistent with democracy. Usury has been viewed with hostility and suspicion. Such ideas were prevalent in presently developing countries during their stagnation phase in the colonial or monarchical eras. This school of thought may be termed as a negative and hostile approach to development of formal financial systems (Adams 1980; Higgins 1959; Lee, Bohlje, and Nelson 1980; and Williamson 1968). It is now little in vogue.

A second approach, the supply-leading finance policy, perceived finance to play a proactive role in economic development. It visualized "the creation of financial institutions and extension of their financial assets, liabilities, and related financial services in advance of demand for them, especially the demand from entrepreneurs in the modern, growth-inducing sectors" (Patrick 1966, 175).[3] According to the policy implications of this view, "Financial intermediation which transfers resources from traditional sectors, whether by collecting wealth and saving from these sectors in exchange for its deposits and financial liabilities or by credit creation and forced saving, is akin to the Schumpeterian concept of innovation financing" (Patrick 1966, 176).

Patrick (1966, 17) further notes that "it cannot be stated that supply-leading finance is a necessary condition or precondition for inaugurating self-sustained economic development. Rather, it presents an opportunity to induce real growth by financial means. It is, thus, likely to play a more significant role at the beginning of the growth process than later." In other words, finance is perceived to play a catalytic role in inducing development of commodity-producing sectors.

A third approach of demand-following finance perceived financial policy to play a mainly neutral and passive role in overall development. Patrick (1966, 174) states that ". . . where enterprise leads, finance follows," and refers to it as the demand-following financial policy. According to this, the evolution of the financial system is a consequence of economic development.

A fourth, hybrid approach of financial policy where supply interacts with demand perceives the role of finance in promoting economic development as resulting from both the demand for and supply of financial services. Patrick (1966, 177) articulates this as follows:

> In actual practice, there is likely to be an interaction of supply-leading and demand-following phenomena. Nevertheless, the following sequence may be postulated. Before sustained modern industrial growth gets underway, supply-leading finance may be able to induce real innovative-type investment. As the process of real growth occurs, the supply-leading impetus gradually becomes less important and the demand-following financial response becomes dominant.

Mellor (1966, 1976) has synthesized the supply-leading and demand-following role of finance for economic development and agricultural development in particular. In his perception, institutional finance should accompany or closely follow programs of technical change. He is clear, however, that institutional finance will fail if it is not closely associated with innovation that increases factor productivity in agriculture. In this context, it must be kept in mind that developing RFIs takes time; therefore, need must be anticipated and early action taken.

---

[3]This paper has at times been classified as advocating demand-following finance, and at other times as recommending supply-leading finance (Adams 1977; Olu 1985; Vogel 1981).

9

Selection of Theme and Issues for Analysis

This analysis focuses on a carefully selected subset of the virtually unlimited total set of rural financial issues. It does so in the context of a potentially technologically dynamic rural sector. Consideration of overall public policy for agricultural development addresses technological, economic, and institutional constraints to development. Agricultural credit policy largely concentrates on relaxing institutional constraint so that a nationally integrated rural financial market can facilitate growth in private investment as well as financial deepening of the rural sector. Such growth induces adoption of new technological and economic opportunities and thereby interacts with the remaining two constraints to agricultural development. This study centers around two broad instruments of agricultural credit policy: deliberate promotion of RFIs and maintenance of interest rates that are conducive to the contribution of these institutions to agricultural growth with equity. This is accomplished by cross-national analysis of the following questions:

- Why promote RFIs? What is the historical experience in this regard (Chapter 3)?
- What organizational principles are needed to encourage successful RFIs? Do such RFIs exist? Are they emerging (Chapters 3-5)?
- What are the transaction costs of RFIs? Are they viable and sustainable? If not, why (Chapter 5)?
- What is the impact of real interest rates and nonprice factors on farmers' demand for loans (Chapter 6), supply of rural deposits (Chapter 7), and supply of rural saving (Chapter 8)?
- What determines the extent to which the institutional rural financial system is a net contributor to or drain on public resources (Chapter 9)?
- What conclusions and implications follow from the analysis of the above questions to improve the developmental impact of RFIs and to achieve the scale economies in transaction costs necessary to their viability (Chapter 10)?

The genesis for the selection of these issues lies in the critical importance of studying underlying strategic management decisions rather than the systemic and procedural aspects of these decisions. It is also in response to current conventional wisdom on the demand-following and strongly neoclassical orientation to rural financial policy (Adams 1977; Gonzalez-Vega 1986). With respect to this neoclassical orientation, the analysis tests the appropriateness of the following central premises of the frequently recommended demand-following finance and the deterministic role of interest rate policy for the rural sector:

- The need for institutional rural finance is very limited; hence, what is required is a minimum number of RFIs, together with traditional, informal lenders taking a proactive role.

- Transaction costs of extending rural credit by RFIs are high and rising. These costs eventually lead to losses, making them inefficient and unviable. They also lack voluntary mobilization of rural deposits and delinquency rates are high.
- Response of rural loan demand is highly inelastic to the real interest rate.
- Response of supply of rural financial deposits to the real interest rate is positive and highly elastic.
- Response of supply of rural saving (physical and financial) to the real interest rate is also positive and highly elastic.

This study tests these premises by reviewing the available literature and further processing data wherever feasible. It then proceeds to alternative causes of existing problems of RFIs' viability and contribution to agricultural development and suggests positive policy alternatives.

Data Sources, Methodology, and Their Strengths and Weaknesses

There is now a tremendous wealth of experience in developing countries regarding development of RFIs. A large literature exists, including extensive description and massive amounts of quantitative data. Dale Adams and his colleagues at Ohio State University have done much to develop, collect, and codify that vast literature. These studies are largely at the country or institutional level. The issues are complex, and the variables are far larger than even the large number of studies that can be drawn on. Thus, a comparative, cross-national analysis can rely only in small part on the rigor of standard statistical tests. A more than normal appeal to judgment is necessary. Nevertheless, the authors have tried to array the evidence carefully so that the reader can evaluate their judgments.

The methodology of this study starts with a large number of country and institutional cases and then pursues three elements. First is a critical review of the published and unpublished literature. Second is further processing and analysis of the data and information given in this literature. This is especially done in chapters related to issues on promotion of RFIs and the impact of real interest rates and nonprice factors on rural loan demand and rural deposit and saving supplies. And third, 13 brief case studies, mostly on Asia, are prepared to cover the issues on transaction costs, scale economies, viability, and developmental effects of RFIs.

A distinctive feature of these case studies is that obtaining economies of scale and scope (that is, savings resulting from the volume and composition of business) in transaction costs is considered an alternative to raising interest rates in order to improve the viability of RFIs. This is important because such economies reflect more efficient use of managerial resources than are common to most activities of RFIs. Also, the case studies provide an opportunity to observe how RFIs use these managerial resources to diversify their lending and nonlending operations. Of the large number of studies under review, only two addressed this issue directly (B. M. Desai 1986b; Desai and Namboodiri 1991).

The issue of scale economies is vital to much of the analysis and is pursued at length in this study. A particular effort was made to quantify the relationships through use of a cost function that relates costs to scale of operation, particularly at the branch level.

For studying other issues, some literature referenced used tabular analysis; other references were based on econometric or programming methods. Further processing and analysis of data mainly relies on quotations from existing literature and econometric and tabular methods. Quotations are used because quantitative information is not available and to further strengthen inferences drawn from the quantitative information that is available. Many of these quotations have been assembled as a supplement to this report, available on request from the International Food Policy Research Institute.

The broad methodological approach used here is cross-national comparisons based on both cross-sectional-sample and time-series data. The limitations of such comparisons are well known. They include different initial conditions and stages of development of RFIs. To reduce the standard problem of noncomparability that plagues cross-sectional studies, some classifications are grouped according to geographical regions and per capita real national income groups. Cross-national comparisons do provide a basis for judging where there is variation in the systems and where there tend to be clear central tendencies.

Because of major differences in coverage of the various sources, the analysis of issues in various chapters does not include the same countries. For example, analysis of institutional finance in Chapters 3 and 4 covers a large number of developed and developing countries, but this is not the case in other chapters. Similarly, the time spans and sizes of cross-sectional samples covered, especially in the chapters on rural loan demand, rural deposits, and rural saving for various countries, lack uniformity. For example, data on these aspects for a country like the United States cover a longer period, from the late 1920s to the 1960s. But for other countries, they cover a shorter period in the 1960s to 1970s or are one- or two-year surveys of cross-sectional households. Lastly, data quality might not be uniform in various studies under review. These limitations are inevitable because the literature on which the present study is based does not uniformly cover issues, nations, sample sizes, and time spans.

3

The Historical Record and Organizational Structure of Formal Rural Financial Institutions

Rural financial market development is a complex process. Review of the literature suggests analysis of that development in terms of the following six organizational principles:

- More than one formal RFI in an area should be promoted.
- A variety of forms of institutions—public, private, and cooperative—should be encouraged.
- The organizational structure should be vertical, proceeding from local to regional to national levels.
- High geographic density of field-level RFIs should be encouraged—that is, a large number of branches, with a small area per branch.
- A large proportion of rural people should be covered by these institutions.
- Diversified and multiple functions should be promoted, that is, functions should be horizontally integrated.

The first two of these organizational principles are analyzed in this chapter and the remaining four are discussed in the next chapter. Prior to that the rationale for rural credit is briefly presented, and the cross-national historical record of growth in the system of RFIs is presented.

Rationale for Rural Finance

Credit is essential for agricultural development. Circumstantial evidence shows that where agriculture has grown rapidly, institutional credit has expanded more quickly. Although farmers as producers greatly prefer to hold their savings in physical productive assets on their own farms, they must also rely on external credit at various points in time, generally because the realization of income and the act of expenditure do not occur at the same time. To cite a few illustrations: A field-crop farmer harvests his crop once or twice a year, whereas his consumption is continuous. For a dairy farmer, the interval between the realization of income and the act of expenditure is shorter and his income is more or less continuous, provided he has two milk animals and ready access to marketing facilities. For a tree-crop farmer, there is a vast gap between the times when expenditure is incurred and when income is generated.

12

There is also a problem of indivisibility of fixed capital—for example, construction of wells; purchase of pumpsets, farm implements, bullocks, and tractors; and improvement of soil and moisture availability all require large expenditures that cannot be divided into smaller payments unless credit is available.

However, far more important than these reasons are the stochastic surges in capital needs and savings that accompany technological innovation in agriculture. In order to shift production functions upward, farmers must be able to purchase modern inputs such as high-yielding varieties of seeds, fertilizers, and irrigation (B. M. Desai 1989; Mellor 1966). Thus, RFIs should promote both credit and deposit services: credit to tide farmers over the deficit period and to enable them to take advantage of the new technological opportunities, and deposit services for savings during periods of surplus. Those surges in agriculture indicate a growth in credit needs for which the elasticity provided by a national or even international credit market is required. The same applies to deposit mobilization when a savings surge follows an investment surge.

Rationale for Institutional Lenders

Nationally integrated financial institutions are necessary and desirable to accomplish financial intermediation between surplus and deficit units, seasons, years, regions, and economic subsystems for agricultural development (Adams 1980; McKinnon 1973; Mellor 1976; Von Pischke, Adams, and Donald 1983). Institutional rural finance in developed as well as developing countries began prior to the time when these countries achieved freedom from colonial or monarchical rule. The following reasons have been cited in the literature for the increase in the role of formal lenders relative to informal lenders in the process of economic development.[4]

- Monetization offers advantages (Bhatt 1983; Long 1983; Reserve Bank of India 1954).
- A widely dispersed agriculture with uneven availability of new technology induces increased demand for and supply of capital (Mellor 1966, 1976; Rosen 1975).
- Weather instability and low and static income of farmers increases demand (Bauer 1952; India, Government of, 1928; Habibulah 1982).
- Finances required for redemption of old debt increased during the interwar period and the Great Depression, which may have relevance though on a smaller scale even now (Agabin 1985; APRACA 1983; Bauer 1952; B. M. Desai 1989; Johnston and Kilby 1975; Rosen 1975).

---

[4]Formal lenders include governments, public institutions, and private institutions such as commercial banks. Informal lenders are shopkeepers, merchants, middlemen, landlords, moneylenders, relatives, and friends.

- Finances are required to confer ownership rights to former tenants under land reform (Agricultural Finance Corporation 1988; APRACA 1983; Bauer 1952; Belshaw 1959; Thailand, Cooperatives Promotion Department 1979; B. M. Desai 1989; Donald 1976; Firth and Yamey 1964; FAO 1973, 1974a, 1974b, 1975, 1976; Mears 1974; Murray 1961; Reserve Bank of India 1945, 1992).
- Because resources of informal lenders are inadequate and ill-suited for modernization, they are unable to lend for long enough periods for farmers to acquire productive assets and market-purchased modern yield-increasing inputs. Hence, the growth of informal lenders has been inelastic (Bauer 1952; Belshaw 1959; Lele 1974; Mears 1974; Mellor 1976; Rosegrant and Siamwalla 1988; Rosen 1975).
- Informal lenders have not been able to mobilize financial deposits because their deposit facilities are inadequate, unsafe, untrustworthy, or less remunerative (B. M. Desai 1989; Donald 1976; Von Pischke, Adams, and Donald 1983).
- The informal credit market is fragmented, imperfect, and isolated (Bauer 1952; Belshaw 1959; B. M. Desai 1976; Firth and Yamey 1964; Nisbet 1969; Reserve Bank of India 1945, 1951).

The extent to which each of these reasons holds for different countries varies, but three conclusions are clear. First, the reasons are essentially universal. Second, they have emerged from the three basic policy goals of RFIs, namely, rural growth with equity, integration of rural financial markets, and economies of scale and scope. And third, the experience of a secular increase in the relative role of institutional credit and the consequent decline in noninstitutional loans has occurred in a wide variety of countries in both developing and developed regions (Figures 1 and 2).

Based on time-series data for nine major Asian countries, Figure 1 shows, first, that the share of institutional loans in the total amount of loans to farm households increased over time in high-income countries (HICs), middle-income countries (MICs), and low-income countries (LICs) in Asia. Second, considering these nine Asian countries at a comparable stage of development, the average share of institutional loans in the present HICs (Japan, Taiwan, the Republic of Korea) was generally higher in the early 1950s and 1960s (an average of about 31 percent) than in the present LICs (the remaining six countries) in the early 1970s (about 19 percent). Third, the increase in the percentage of institutional loans over time was much higher in Asian MICs (except Taiwan) and Asian LICs than in Japan or Taiwan. This is because the Asian MICs had a much lower share of institutional loans to begin with. Moreover, between Japan and Taiwan, the increase in the institutional share was sharper in Taiwan. Both these facts suggest that initial conditions related to RFIs were much more favorable in Japan than in the LICs. This is also true for Taiwan, followed by the Republic of Korea, and the Philippines.

Cross-national shares of institutional loans in the mid- to late-1970s reinforce the above conclusions (Figure 2). The share of institutional

Figure 1—Share of borrowing of farm households from institutional and noninstitutional sources, selected Asian countries, various years

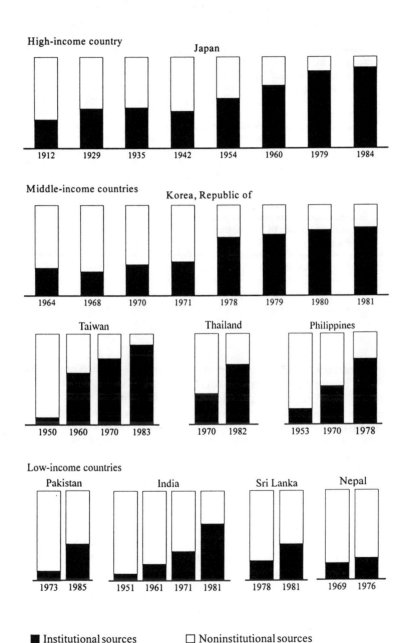

■ Institutional sources   □ Noninstitutional sources

Figure 1—Continued

Sources: Brake et al. 1971; Donald 1976; Pakistan, Government of, 1974; Kato 1966, 1984; D. H. Lee 1984; Malik 1989; Reserve Bank of India 1992.

Notes: For Japan, institutional loans are from special banks, ordinary commercial banks, insurance companies, individual cooperative associations (agricultural cooperative associations), simplified government insurance system, and government; for the Republic of Korea, from agricultural cooperatives, rural banks, commercial banks, mutual savings and loan banks, credit associations, and insurance companies; for Taiwan, from government-owned banks, agricultural cooperatives, and farmers' associations; for Thailand, from government-owned banks, agricultural cooperatives/farmers' associations, commercial banks, mutual savings and loan banks, credit associations, and insurance companies; for the Philippines, from government, government-owned banks, and rural banks; for India, from agricultural cooperatives, nationalized commercial banks, and regional rural banks; for Pakistan, from government and government-owned banks; and for Nepal and Sri Lanka, from government-owned banks, agricultural cooperatives, and commercial banks.

For Japan, noninstitutional loans are from individual moneylenders, pawn shops, merchants, loan companies, mutual saving associations, and individuals; for the Republic of Korea, from professional moneylenders, relatives, friends, informal groups, individuals, *kye*, traders and merchants, agriculturalists, and manufacturers and processors; for Taiwan, from merchants, informal groups, *Hui*, individuals, and others; for Thailand and the Philippines, from landlords, merchants, professional moneylenders, and individuals; for India, from agricultural moneylenders, professional moneylenders, traders and commission agents, landlords and tenants, and relatives; and for Pakistan, Nepal, and Sri Lanka, from landlords, merchants, professional moneylenders, pawn shops, and individuals.

loans increases with the increase in opportunities to raise per capita real national income and especially rural income within a given region. This is found for Sub-Saharan African LICs (7 percent) versus MICs (40 percent), as well as for South Asian LICs (20 percent) versus Southeast Asian MICs (44 percent) versus Asian HICs (86 percent).

The share of institutional loans across countries and regions is positively associated with the opportunities to raise per capita real national income and institutional development. This follows from the comparison of these shares among African LICs (7 percent), Asian LICs (20 percent), Asian MICs (44 percent), an Asian HIC (86 percent), Near East and Mediterranean Basin MICs (49 percent), Latin American and the Caribbean MICs (70-96 percent),[5] and a North American HIC (over 75 percent). The very small shares of noninstitutional loans in some Latin American and Caribbean countries is perhaps due to the lack of a tradition of informal moneylending in these countries.

---

[5]The extremely high share of RFIs in Latin America and the Caribbean may not be interpreted to suggest that RFIs have reached a larger proportion of farmers in that region. In fact, this is not the case, as will be shown in the next chapter. Nor is it true that these countries have lower transaction costs, as will be shown in Chapter 5.

17

Figure 2—Share of agricultural loans from institutional and noninstitutional sources in selected countries and regions

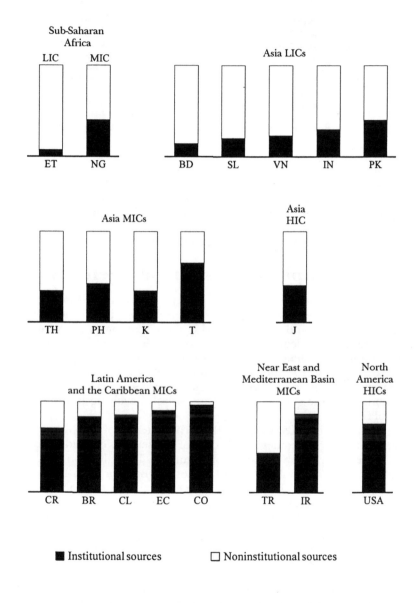

■ Institutional sources   □ Noninstitutional sources

Sources: Brake et al. 1971; Donald 1976; Pakistan, Government of, 1974; Kato 1966, 1984; D. H. Lee 1984; Malik 1989; Reserve Bank of India 1992.
Notes: In the United States, the share of noninstitutional sources includes loans made by the Small Business Administration Association, which is a formal autonomous government agency.

Figure 2—Continued

LIC is low-income countries, MIC is middle-income countries, and HIC is high-income countries.

ET	= Ethiopia	T	= Taiwan
NG	= Nigeria (West)	J	= Japan
BD	= Bangladesh	CR	= Costa Rica
SL	= Sri Lanka	BR	= Brazil
VN	= Republic of Vietnam	CL	= Chile
IN	= India	EC	= Ecuador
PK	= Pakistan	CO	= Colombia
TH	= Thailand	TR	= Turkey
PH	= Philippines	IR	= Iran
K	= Republic of Korea	USA	= United States

The share of institutional loans is significantly higher in Asian LICs than in African LICs. This may be due to early development of an institutional framework for rural finance, which became possible because of more and better-trained workers in the Asian countries. It is also due to an earlier emphasis on promoting the role of agriculture for economic development in Asian LICs than in African LICs.

Multiple Versus Single Agencies

Should there be one or more than one type of formal RFI in a country? There are several arguments against multiple agencies, including loss of scale economies and fears that having more than one agency may lead to more than one loan of the same type to one farmer. There is little or no empirical evidence to support this fear. But the single-agency approach can lead to monopoly, with all of its associated disadvantages. Review of the literature provides the following generalizations, representing both the supply and demand sides of evolving institutions for rural finance.

Increases in and changes in the term structure of loan demand and deposit supply schedules make some of the services offered by existing RFIs inappropriate (Donald 1976; Izumida 1988; Kahlon and Singh 1984; Kato 1970; Mellor 1966, 1976; Reserve Bank of India 1969; Rosen 1975; World Bank 1973). Some of the existing RFIs may lack comparative advantage because the term structure of their loanable resources is ill-suited to serve the rural poor or more difficult agricultural areas (Aku 1986; Colyer and Jimenez 1971; Green 1983; Hussi and Abbott 1973; Kato 1970; D. H. Lee 1984; J. H. Lee 1984; Murray 1961; Reserve Bank of India 1969; Rosen 1975). The increasing availability of trained people over time facilitates the growth of a wide range of financial services. Indeed, historical experience shows that the process of promoting formal RFIs begins with one agency and evolves into multiagencies in country after country (Agabin 1988b; Donald 1976; FAO 1973, 1974a, 1974b, 1975, 1976; Lee, Bohlje, and Nelson 1980).

The different types of RFIs considered are government departments and corporations, cooperatives, commercial banks, specialized sector-specific or economy-wide development banks, agrarian reform institutions, and insurance companies. All of the different types that exist in a country have been counted to obtain the number of RFIs of each type in each country.[6] Table 1 shows that multiple RFIs are found in widely diverse situations in Sub-Saharan Africa, Asia, the Near East and Mediterranean Basin, North America, Latin America and the Caribbean, and Western Europe. This is so irrespective of the level of per capita real national income and whether or not the RFI system is successful, as it has been in Japan, the Republic of Korea, Taiwan, and the United States.

Furthermore, in 81 out of the 98 countries included, there are more than two types of RFIs. The exceptions are five African LICs (Chad, Dahomey, Niger, Togo, and Upper Volta), four African MICs (Congo, Côte d'Ivoire, Gabon, and Senegal), one Asian LIC (Nepal), one Near East and Mediterranean Basin HIC (Libya), and one Latin American and Caribbean MIC (Cuba), and two each in the Near East and Mediterranean Basin MICs (Egypt and Turkey), and West European HICs (United Kingdom and Germany).

Forms of Organization of RFIs

What form of organization should RFIs take? Should they be government agencies, autonomous public agencies, private agencies, cooperatives, or specialized public agencies for the rural sector? The process of promoting RFIs typically begins with government departments or cooperatives. Commercial banks are normally reluctant to enter the rural financial market, mainly because of initial problems of scale and the difficulty of supervising small, dispersed branches. Cooperatives are preferred for two additional reasons. First, farmers themselves manage their own institutions and thereby the process makes a smaller claim on scarce managerial resources. And second, farmers' involvement means community participation, which in turn leads to better knowledge of borrowers and to democratic decisionmaking (Jones 1971).

As experience was gained with cooperatives, it became clear that institutionalizing rural credit is a highly complex procedure. It requires not only the disbursal of credit of the right kind at the right time, but also specialized and democratic management structures and skills to run the institution. The policy response consisted of two instruments (Donald 1976; Jones 1971; Youngjohns 1983). First, supervised credit and development of access to inputs and marketing facilities were introduced to tackle the former of these two tasks—disbursal of credit. And second, personnel of the existing RFIs were trained to tackle both credit and management problems. But cooperatives often lacked the ability and perhaps the intent to fulfill their basic goals; they generally did not succeed in serving the rural poor (Illy 1983; Jones 1971; Murray 1961).

---

[6]Commodity-based marketing institutions that merely transfer government funds to farmers in the form of inputs and recover them by purchasing their produce are excluded. These are more prevalent in Sub-Saharan Africa and Latin America and the Caribbean, particularly for perishable and semiperishable export crops.

Table 1—Number of rural financial institutions (RFIs) in developing and developed countries selected for the study, mid-1970s

Region, Country, and Income Group	Number of RFIs	Region, Country, and Income Group	Number of RFIs
Sub-Saharan Africa		High-income country	
Low-income countries		Japan	8
Burundi	3	Near East and Mediterranean	
Central African Republic	3	Basin	
Chad	2	Low-income countries	
Dahomey	2	Afghanistan	3
Ethiopia	4	Sudan	5
The Gambia	4	Middle-income countries	
Madagascar	4	Cyprus	4
Malawi	3	Egypt	2
Mali	3	Iran	3
Mauritania	4	Jordan	3
Niger	2	Morocco	3
Rwanda	4	Syria	3
Sierra Leone	4	Tunisia	3
Tanzania	3	Turkey	2
Togo	1	High-income countries	
Uganda	4	Libya	2
Upper Volta	2	Saudi Arabia	3
Zaire	4	Latin America and the Caribbean	
Middle-income countries		Low-income countries	
Botswana	4	Bolivia	5
Cameroon	3	Guyana	4
Congo	2	Haiti	3
Côte d'Ivoire	2	Middle-income countries	
Gabon	1	Argentina	3
Ghana	4	Barbados	4
Kenya	4	Belize	4
Lesotho	3	Brazil	5
Liberia	4	Chile	7
Mauritius	4	Colombia	6
Nigeria	5	Costa Rica	4
Senegal	2	Cuba	1
Swaziland	3	Dominica	4
Zambia	4	Dominican Republic	4
Asia		Ecuador	6
Low-income countries		El Salvador	6
Bangladesh	5	Grenada	3
Burma	3	Guatemala	4
China, Peoples' Republic of	3	Honduras	3
India	4	Jamaica	4
Indonesia	3	Martinique	3
Khmer Republic	3	Mexico	4
Nepal	2	Nicaragua	5
Pakistan	4	Panama	3
Sri Lanka	4	Paraguay	4
Middle-income countries		Peru	5
Korea, Republic of	4	Surinam	3
Malaysia	9	Trinidad and Tobago	4
Philippines	6	Turks and Caicos	3
Thailand	4	Uruguay	3
Taiwan	7	Venezuela	6

(continued)

Table 1—Continued

Region, Country, and Income Group	Number of RFIs	Region, Country, and Income Group	Number of RFIs
North America[a]		France	4
High-income country		Germany	2
United States	10	Ireland	3
Western Europe[a]		Italy	8
High-income countries		Netherlands	4
Belgium	3	United Kingdom	2
Denmark	4		

Sources: FAO 1973, 1974a, 1974b, 1975, 1976; Lee, Bohlje, and Nelson 1980; Ruozi 1979.
Notes: The RFIs considered here are primarily financial institutions and exclude commodity-based marketing institutions. The numbers do not refer to the number of units (or branches) of each type of RFI.
[a]For North America and Western Europe, the number of RFIs refers to the late-1970s.

This led to the emergence of state-sponsored specialized banks in many countries in Africa, Asia, the Near East and Mediterranean Basin, and Latin America and the Caribbean. Some countries, such as Bangladesh, India, and the Philippines, pursued state-owned or state-supported commercial banks or nationalization of the existing major commercial banks or both. The emergence of new institutions did not mean discontinuation of the old institutions, for they were well entrenched in the socioeconomic polity of the rural sector. This is so in many developing as well as developed countries.

Thus historical experience again shows that all forms of organization are found world over (Table 2). Moreover, public institutions are ubiquitous even in later stages of development, as seen in Japan, the Republic of Korea, Taiwan, and the United States (Agabin 1988b; Colyer and Jimenez 1971; Egaitsu 1988b; Izumida 1988; Jones 1971; Lee, Bohlje, and Nelson 1980). Even cooperatives and private commercial banks do not initially enter the rural capital market without sustained government support in all of the six major regions of the world.

There are, however, some important differences among RFIs in various countries (Table 2). First, the share of government corporations, projects, and departments in the total number of RFIs is higher in Sub-Saharan Africa, the Near East and Mediterranean Basin, and Latin America and the Caribbean than in other regions. This type of institutional arrangement is less useful in the long run because it is transient and hence cannot build the specialized institutional capacity and the professionalism so critical to the development of RFIs. The high shares of government programs in Japan, the Republic of Korea, and Taiwan, however, do not contradict this statement because, unlike those in the aforementioned regions, these government institutions are well integrated with the other types of RFIs. Second, although the shares of cooperatives in Africa and Latin America are fairly comparable to those in other regions, it should not be assumed that this form of RFI in these two regions is well developed. These cooperatives are either local or

Table 2—Share of different types of organization of rural
financial institutions in the total number, mid-1970s

Region, Country, and Income Group	Government National Banks, Agricultural Banks, or Financing Agencies	National-ized Commercial Banks	Private Commercial or Savings Banks	Coopera-tive Banks or Local Coopera-tives	Government Corpora-tions, Projects or Depart-ments
			(percent)		
Sub-Saharan Africa					
Low-income countries					
Burundi	33.0	. . .	67.0	. . .	. . .
Central African Republic	. . .	33.3	33.3	. . .	33.4
Chad	50.0	. . .	50.0	. . .	. . .
Dahomey	50.0	. . .	50.0	. . .	. . .
Ethiopia	25.0	25.0	25.0	25.0[a]	. . .
The Gambia	. . .	25.0	25.0	25.0[a]	25.0
Madagascar	25.0	. . .	25.0	25.0	25.0
Malawi	. . .	. . .	33.3	33.3[a]	33.4
Mali	. . .	. . .	33.3	33.3[a]	33.4
Mauritania	25.0	. . .	25.0	25.0[a]	25.0
Niger	50.0	. . .	50.0	. . .	. . .
Rwanda	25.0	. . .	50.0	25.0[a]	. . .
Sierra Leone	25.0	. . .	25.0	25.0	25.0
Tanzania	67.0	33.0	. . .	. . .	. . .
Togo	100.0	. . .	. . .	. . .	. . .
Uganda	25.0	25.0	25.0	25.0	. . .
Upper Volta	50.0	. . .	. . .	. . .	50.0
Zaire	25.0	. . .	25.0	25.0[a]	. . .
Average	26.8	8.9	30.3	17.9	16.1
Middle-income countries					
Botswana	25.0	. . .	25.0	50.0[a]	. . .
Cameroon	67.0	. . .	. . .	33.0[a]	. . .
Congo	50.0	. . .	50.0	. . .	. . .
Côte d'Ivoire	50.0	. . .	50.0	. . .	. . .
Gabon	100.0	. . .	. . .	. . .	. . .
Ghana	50.0	. . .	25.0	25.0[a]	. . .
Kenya	25.0	. . .	25.0	25.0	25.0
Lesotho	33.3	. . .	. . .	33.3	33.4
Liberia	25.0	. . .	25.0	25.0[a]	25.0
Mauritius	25.0	25.0	25.0	25.0	. . .
Nigeria	40.0	. . .	20.0	20.0	20.0
Senegal	50.0	. . .	. . .	50.0[a]	. . .
Swaziland	33.3	. . .	33.3	. . .	33.4
Zambia	50.0	. . .	25.0	25.0[a]	. . .
Average	40.0	2.2	22.3	24.4	11.1
Asia					
Low-income countries					
Bangladesh	40.0	20.0	. . .	20.0	20.0
Burma	100.0	. . .	. . .	. . .	. . .
China, Peoples' Republic of	33.3	33.3	. . .	33.4	. . .
India	25.0	25.0	. . .	50.0	. . .
Indonesia	33.3	. . .	33.3	33.4[a]	. . .
Khmer Republic	67.0	. . .	33.0	. . .	. . .
Nepal	50.0	. . .	50.0	. . .	. . .

(continued)

Table 2—Continued

Region, Country, and Income Group	Government National Banks, Agricultural Banks, or Financing Agencies	National-ized Com-mercial Banks	Private Commer-cial or Savings Banks	Coopera-tive Banks or Local Coopera-tives	Govern-ment Corpora-tions, Projects or Depart-ments
			(percent)		
Pakistan	25.0	25.0	. . .	25.0	25.0
Sri Lanka	50.0	25.0	. . .	25.0[a]	. . .
Average	45.2	16.1	9.7	22.6	6.4
Middle-income countries					
Korea, Republic of	. . .	. . .	25.0	50.0	25.0
Malaysia	22.2	. . .	22.2	22.2[a]	33.4
Philippines	50.0	. . .	33.3	16.7[a]	. . .
Taiwan	28.6	. . .	. . .	28.6	42.8
Thailand	. . .	. . .	25.0	75.0[a]	. . .
Average	23.3	. . .	20.0	33.3	23.4
Average of Taiwan and Korea	18.2	. . .	9.1	36.4	36.3
Average of Malaysia and the Philippines	26.3	. . .	26.3	31.6	15.8
High-income country					
Japan	12.5	. . .	12.5	12.5	62.5
Near East and Mediterranean Basin					
Low-income countries					
Afghanistan	33.3	. . .	33.3	. . .	33.4
Sudan	20.0	. . .	40.0	20.0	20.0
Average	25.0	. . .	37.5	12.5	25.0
Middle-income countries					
Cyprus	. . .	. . .	25.0	50.0	25.0
Egypt	. . .	. . .	50.0	50.0	. . .
Iran	. . .	. . .	33.3	33.3	33.4
Jordan	33.3	. . .	33.3	33.4	. . .
Morocco	33.3	. . .	33.3	. . .	33.4
Syria	. . .	. . .	33.3	33.3	33.4
Tunisia	33.3	. . .	33.3	. . .	33.4
Turkey	50.0	. . .	50.0	. . .	. . .
Average	17.4	. . .	34.8	26.1	21.7
High-income countries					
Libya	50.0	50.0	. . .	. . .	. . .
Saudi Arabia	33.3	. . .	33.3	. . .	33.4
Average	40.0	20.0	20.0	. . .	20.0
North America					
High-income country					
United States	30.0	. . .	40.0	30.0	. . .
Latin America and the Caribbean					
Middle-income countries					
Argentina	. . .	. . .	33.3	66.7[b]	. . .
Barbados	75.0	. . .	25.0	. . .	. . .
Belize	25.0	. . .	25.0	50.0[b]	. . .
Brazil	20.0	40.0	20.0	20.0	. . .
Chile	14.3	. . .	14.3	14.3	57.1
Colombia	50.0	. . .	33.3	. . .	16.7

(continued)

Table 2—Continued

Region, Country, and Income Group	Government National Banks, Agricultural Banks, or Financing Agencies	National-ized Commercial Banks	Private Commercial or Savings Banks	Cooperative Banks or Local Cooperatives	Government Corporations, Projects or Departments
			(percent)		
Costa Rica	25.0	25.0	25.0	25.0	...
Cuba	100.0	...	...	...	...
Dominica	25.0	...	25.0	50.0[b]	...
Dominican Republic	25.0	...	25.0	25.0[b]	25.0
Ecuador	33.3	...	16.7	33.3	16.7
El Salvador	16.7	...	33.3	33.3	16.7
Grenada	33.3	...	33.3	33.4	...
Guatemala	25.0	...	25.0	25.0[b]	25.0
Honduras	33.3	...	33.3	33.4	...
Jamaica	25.0	...	25.0	25.0	25.0
Martinique	...	...	33.3	66.7[b]	...
Mexico	25.0	...	50.0	25.0[b]	...
Nicaragua	20.0	...	40.0	20.0[b]	20.0
Panama	33.3	...	33.3	33.4	...
Paraguay	25.0	...	25.0	25.0[b]	25.0
Peru	20.0	...	40.0	20.0	20.0
Surinam	66.7	...	33.3	...	...
Trinidad and Tobago	25.0	...	25.0	50.0[b]	...
Turks and Caicos	...	...	33.3	33.3[b]	33.4
Uruguay	33.3	...	33.3	33.4	...
Venezuela	50.0	...	33.3	...	16.7
Average	28.8	2.8	28.8	26.1	13.5
Western Europe					
High-income countries					
Belgium	66.7	...	...	33.3	...
Denmark	...	...	50.0	50.0	...
France	50.0	...	25.0	25.0	...
Germany, Federal Republic of	50.0	...	...	50.0	...
Ireland	66.7	...	33.3	...	...
Italy	...	12.5	25.0	37.5	25.0
Netherlands	...	...	25.0	75.0	...
United Kingdom	50.0	...	50.0	...	...
Average	26.7	3.3	26.7	36.7	6.6

Sources: FAO 1973, 1974a, 1974b, 1975, 1976; Lee, Bohlje, and Nelson 1980; Ruozi 1979.
[a]These are for local cooperatives without their federations.
[b]Half of these are for local cooperatives without their federations.

regional without higher or lower levels of organization. Third, government-sponsored specialized development banks (sector-specific or all sectors) are found in all six regions, including the United States and Western Europe. Fourth, the same holds true for commercial banks, although nationalized commercial banks are more common in Asian LICs and to some extent in African LICs.

Despite these differences, whether public or private RFIs will perform better cannot be judged a priori. Historical experiences show that both have coexisted with sustained government support of one type or another. Moreover, even though there may be a need to initiate formal rural finance through a government department, longer-term considerations require that these functions be transferred to existing RFIs or that autonomous participative institutions be created with their own basic financial operations for agricultural development. Such RFIs should also be vertically integrated, spread out to cover a large number of areas and rural households, and multifunctional in their operations. The next chapter analyzes specific policies for promoting formal RFIs.

4

Vertical Integration, Density of Coverage, and Multiproduct Structure of Formal Rural Financial Institutions

The remaining four organizational principles of the six stated in Chapter 3 for developing RFIs are critical to attaining three basic goals of agricultural credit policy: rural growth with equity, integration of rural financial markets, and economies of scale and scope for viability of formal RFIs.

Vertical Organization of Various Types of RFIs

Should different types of RFIs be vertically integrated from their local units to regional and national levels? Vertically organized RFIs are better able to integrate regional and national financial markets, to provide managerial guidance to their lower-level units, to arrive at a more interactive understanding for strategic decisions, and to decentralize implementation processes for rural finance operations. Such internal management structures can lead to more effective and efficient mobilization and utilization of both financial and human capital. They also facilitate identification and implementation of opportunities for financial intermediation geared to specific situations.

Without vertical integration, internal economies of scale in financial and transaction costs cannot be reaped, with consequent adverse implications for viability. Such RFIs tend to be less useful to farmers and other rural clients because of the irregularity and inadequacy of their services. Local cooperatives without regional or national federations cannot survive long unless they have adequate financial resources and professional management.

Cross-national information to identify the qualitative features of vertically integrated RFIs is weak to nonexistent. However, whether an RFI has its constituents at various levels (apex, intermediate, and local) can be broadly approximated from the available literature. On that ground and on the basis of observations, availability of the types of capabilities that vertically organized RFIs have appears weak in Africa, the Near East and Mediterranean Basin, and Latin America and the

Caribbean, compared with Asia. The proportion of RFIs without regional or local organizations or both is highest in Africa, followed by Latin America and the Caribbean, the Near East and Mediterranean Basin, and lastly Asia (Table 3). The share of RFIs lacking vertical organization is higher in LICs than in MICs or HICs, irrespective of region to which the country belongs. Fewer Asian LICs have vertically organized RFIs than Asian MICs. In Taiwan, the Republic of Korea, Japan, and the United States, all of the RFIs are vertically integrated.[7]

Density of Field-level RFIs

Since agriculture is geographically widely dispersed, small-scale, and diverse, there is a clear need for a high density of RFIs. Increasing the density of field-level RFIs is a necessary condition for rural financial market development, transference of new technology for agricultural development, and mobilization of deposits from rural areas.

High density may adversely affect economies of scale, leading to initial losses and occasionally future losses for some local branches. However, it is still important to increase density, because higher densities (1) improve accessibility for both rural households and formal lenders, which in turn generates understanding of specific situations, bringing about improved appraisal, monitoring, and evaluation by RFIs; (2) enable the scope of lending and nonlending operations to be widened and intensified in order to reap scale economies, which are crucial to the spread of the common transaction costs peculiar to RFIs; (3) facilitate effective competition with the informal lenders, thereby enlarging coverage of farmers and other rural households; and (4) reduce the transaction costs of rural borrowers and depositors. Studies that quantify each of these benefits do not exist, although some recent studies have shown that improvement in banking infrastructure does encourage deposit mobilization (Asian Development Bank 1985).

Column 3 in Table 3 reports data on density (the number of field-level RFIs per 1,000 hectares of arable land) for 11 major Asian countries for which data are available. It shows that agricultural development or per capita real national income or both are related to higher density of field-level institutions and hence more developed and successful RFI systems. Successful RFIs are found in all three Asian countries with higher densities (Japan, Taiwan, and the Republic of Korea in that order). Even the People's Republic of China, a major LIC with rapid agricultural growth, may have a more successful RFI system than most Asian MICs (including the Philippines and Thailand) and other Asian

---

[7]This is not to suggest that the RFIs in these countries do not have recurrent problems. For example, in the United States in the 1980s, there were severe financial problems in RFIs. These arose largely from deflation of farm land values with the change in price regime, and in interest rates and deregulation of interest rates. This indicates that public policy should continuously evaluate various changes in the environment to identify appropriate measures to reduce their negative impacts and thereby promote a strong RFI system.

Table 3—Vertical integration, density, and coverage of formal rural financial institutions (RFIs) in selected developing and developed countries

Region, Country, and Income Group	Percent of RFIs Not Vertically Organized[a] (1)	Density of Field-Level RFIs[b] Year (2)	Density (3)	Proportion of Rural People Borrowing from RFIs Year (4)	Percent (5)
Sub-Saharan Africa					
Low-income countries					
Burundi	67	n.a.	n.a.	n.a.	n.a.
Central African Republic	67	n.a.	n.a.	n.a.	n.a.
Chad	50	n.a.	n.a.	n.a.	n.a.
Dahomey	0	n.a.	n.a.	n.a.	n.a.
Ethiopia	50	n.a.	n.a.	1974	1.0
The Gambia	50	n.a.	n.a.	n.a.	n.a.
Madagascar	25	n.a.	n.a.	n.a.	n.a.
Malawi	67	n.a.	n.a.	1974	8.0
Mali	67	n.a.	n.a.	n.a.	n.a.
Mauritania	75	n.a.	n.a.	n.a.	n.a.
Niger	50	n.a.	n.a.	n.a.	n.a.
Rwanda	100	n.a.	n.a.	n.a.	n.a.
Sierra Leone	50	n.a.	n.a.	n.a.	n.a.
Tanzania	33	n.a.	n.a.	1974	4.0
Togo	0	n.a.	n.a.	n.a.	n.a.
Uganda	25	n.a.	n.a.	n.a.	n.a.
Upper Volta	50	n.a.	n.a.	1974	6.0
Zaire	50	n.a.	n.a.	1974	3.0
Average	50	n.a.	n.a.	1974	4.4
Middle-income countries					
Botswana	50	n.a.	n.a.	n.a.	n.a.
Cameroon	33	n.a.	n.a.	n.a.	n.a.
Congo	50	n.a.	n.a.	n.a.	n.a.
Côte d'Ivoire	0	n.a.	n.a.	1974	15.0
Gabon	0	n.a.	n.a.	n.a.	n.a.
Ghana	25	n.a.	n.a.	1974	3.0
Kenya	0	n.a.	n.a.	1974	17.0
Lesotho	33	n.a.	n.a.	1974	6.0
Liberia	25	n.a.	n.a.	n.a.	n.a.
Mauritius	0	n.a.	n.a.	n.a.	n.a.
Nigeria	20	n.a.	n.a.	n.a.	n.a.
Senegal	50	n.a.	n.a.	n.a.	n.a.
Swaziland	0	n.a.	n.a.	n.a.	n.a.
Zambia	25	n.a.	n.a.	n.a.	n.a.
Average	22	n.a.	n.a.	1974	10.3
Asia					
Low-income countries					
Bangladesh	0	1979	0.192	1974	15.0
Burma	0	n.a.	n.a.	n.a.	n.a.
China, Peoples' Republic of	0	1979	3.735	n.a.	n.a.
India	0	1979	0.689	1974	20.0
				1981	25.0
Indonesia	0	1979	0.366	1983	9.0
Khmer Republic	33	n.a.	n.a.	n.a.	n.a.

(continued)

Table 3—Continued

Region, Country, and Income Group	Percent of RFIs Not Vertically Organized[a] (1)	Density of Field-Level RFIs[b]		Proportion of Rural People Borrowing from RFIs	
		Year (2)	Density (3)	Year (4)	Percent (5)
Nepal	50	1979	0.410	1979	24.0
Pakistan	0	n.a.	n.a.	1974	5.0
Sri Lanka	50	1979	0.371	1974	14.0
Average	13	1979 (1979)	0.960 (0.406)[c]	1974	13.5
Middle-income countries					
Korea, Republic of	0	1979	1.112	1974	40.0
Malaysia	11	n.a.	n.a.	1974	2.0
Philippines	17	1980	0.436	1974	28.0
				1979	33.0
Taiwan	0	1979	1.265	1974	95.0
Thailand	25	1980	0.500	1974	7.0
Average	10	1979/80	0.828	1974	34.4
Average for Taiwan and Korea, Republic of	0	1979	1.188	1974	67.5
Average for Philippines and Thailand	16	1980	0.468	1974	17.5
High-income country					
Japan	0	1979	4.611	n.a.	n.a.
Near East and Mediterranean Basin					
Low-income countries					
Afghanistan	0	n.a.	n.a.	n.a.	n.a.
Sudan	20	n.a.	n.a.	1974	1.0
Average	10	n.a.	n.a.	1974	1.0
Middle-income countries					
Cyprus	0	n.a.	n.a.	n.a.	n.a.
Egypt	0	n.a.	n.a.	n.a.	n.a.
Iran	0	n.a.	n.a.	n.a.	n.a.
Jordan	0	n.a.	n.a.	1974	8.0
Morocco	0	n.a.	n.a.	1974	10.0
Syria	0	n.a.	n.a.	n.a.	n.a.
Tunisia	0	n.a.	n.a.	1974	5.0
Turkey	0	n.a.	n.a.	1974	23.0
Average	0	n.a.	n.a.	1974	11.5
High-income countries					
Libya	0	n.a.	n.a.	n.a.	n.a.
Saudi Arabia	0	n.a.	n.a.	n.a.	n.a.
Average	0	n.a.	n.a.	n.a.	n.a.
North America					
High-income country					
United States	0	n.a.	n.a.	n.a.	n.a.
Latin America and the Caribbean					
Low-income countries					
Bolivia	20	n.a.	n.a.	1975	5.0
Guyana	25	n.a.	n.a.	1975	4.0
Haiti	0	n.a.	n.a.	n.a.	n.a.
Average	17	n.a.	n.a.	1975	4.5

(continued)

Table 3—Continued

Region, Country, and Income Group	Percent of RFIs Not Vertically Organized[a] (1)	Density of Field-Level RFIs[b] Year (2)	Density (3)	Proportion of Rural People Borrowing from RFIs Year (4)	Percent (5)
Middle-income countries					
Argentina	33	n.a.	n.a.	n.a.	n.a.
Barbados	0	n.a.	n.a.	n.a.	n.a.
Belize	25	n.a.	n.a.	n.a.	n.a.
Brazil	0	n.a.	n.a.	1975	15.0
Chile	0	n.a.	n.a.	1975	28.0
Colombia	0	n.a.	n.a.	1975	38.0
Costa Rica	0	n.a.	n.a.	n.a.	n.a.
Cuba	0	n.a.	n.a.	n.a.	n.a.
Dominica	25	n.a.	n.a.	n.a.	n.a.
Dominican Republic	25	n.a.	n.a.	1975	14.0
Ecuador	0	n.a.	n.a.	1975	18.0
El Salvador	0	n.a.	n.a.	1975	9.0
Grenada	33	n.a.	n.a.	n.a.	n.a.
Guatemala	25	n.a.	n.a.	1975	2.0
Honduras	0	n.a.	n.a.	1975	10.0
Jamaica	0	n.a.	n.a.	1975	65.0
Martinique	33	n.a.	n.a.	n.a.	n.a.
Mexico	25	n.a.	n.a.	1975	20.0
Nicaragua	20	n.a.	n.a.	1975	20.0
Panama	33	n.a.	n.a.	1975	20.0
Paraguay	25	n.a.	n.a.	1975	4.0
Peru	20	n.a.	n.a.	1975	24.0
Surinam	0	n.a.	n.a.	n.a.	n.a.
Trinidad and Tobago	25	n.a.	n.a.	1975	10.0
Turks and Caicos	67	n.a.	n.a.	n.a.	n.a.
Uruguay	33	n.a.	n.a.	n.a.	n.a.
Venezuela	0	n.a.	n.a.	n.a.	n.a.
Average	14	n.a.	n.a.	1975	22.6

Sources: Asian Productivity Organization 1984, 1985; Donald 1976; FAO 1973, 1974a, 1974b, 1975, 1976; Kato 1966, 1984; Olin 1975; Rangarajan 1974; Reserve Bank of India various issues a, various issues b; and Widayati 1985.

Note: n.a. means not available.

[a]Vertically organized RFIs are those that have regional, national, and local-level institutions.

[b]Density of field-level RFIs is measured as the number of these institutions per 1,000 hectares of arable land.

[c]The Peoples' Republic of China is excluded.

LICs (including Bangladesh, India, Indonesia, Nepal, and Sri Lanka). The correlation between income and density of RFIs is borne out when Asian MICs and LICs are compared (Taiwan and the Republic of Korea as against the Philippines and Thailand, for example; or China, India, Nepal, and Sri Lanka as against Bangladesh and Indonesia).[8]

Two additional observations may be made. First, the countries of North America and Western Europe are likely to have a higher density of field-level RFIs than Japan. And second, many countries in Africa, the Near East and Mediterranean Basin, and Latin America and the Caribbean have very low densities; the proportion of farmers covered by RFIs in these regions is lower than in Asia.

Proportion of Rural Households Reached by an RFI System

The importance of covering a high proportion of rural households cannot be questioned. Agricultural credit policy also aims at larger coverage of rural households not only to meet their credit needs, but also to provide a place to deposit excess liquidity whenever it arises during production and consumption cycles.

The following findings are derived from column 5 in Table 3. First, the share of rural people borrowing from RFIs is higher in MICs than in LICs, no matter in which developing-country region the country is located. Second, for the region as a whole, the share of borrowers is highest in Asia (23.55), followed by Latin America and the Caribbean (20.47), the Near East and Mediterranean Basin (9.40), and Sub-Saharan Africa (6.11). Third, this ordering of the four regions remains unchanged when countries with very high percentages are excluded; Asia (13.78 percent), followed by Latin America and the Caribbean (13.07), then the Near East and Mediterranean Basin (9.40), and lastly Africa (6.11). And fourth, two recently developed Asian MICs, Taiwan and the Republic of Korea, have RFI systems reaching the largest proportion of rural households.[9]

Another policy concern is the proportion of small farmers reached by RFIs. Available data on 17 countries suggest that the share of small farmers reached is highest in Asian MICs (particularly Taiwan), followed

---

[8]In some cases, the association between agricultural growth or per capita real national income and density of RFIs among Asian LICs is not apparent, suggesting that other factors also influence density. These include varied agroclimatic environment, terrain of the country, and size of the rural population. Consequently, strong positive association may not result, particularly in the short- to medium-term period.

[9]This share is, however, lower in the Republic of Korea than in Jamaica or Peru. This may be because the year to which data refer may have extraordinarily low and high figures. Moreover, the Korean RFI system is widely acclaimed as successful, but the Jamaican and Peruvian systems are not (Adams 1988b; Asian Productivity Organization 1984; Brake 1971; Donald 1976; FAO 1974a, 1975; Kato 1984; D. H. Lee 1984; and Olin 1975).

by Asian LICs, the African MIC, and Latin American and Caribbean MICs and LICs (Table 4). It must, however, be noted that these data are incomplete and do not define small farmers uniformly. Nevertheless, the conclusion derived would be unlikely to change dramatically if data were complete.

Table 4—Share of small farmers receiving institutional loans and land in selected developing countries, mid-1970s

Region, Country, and Income Group	Definition of Small Farmers[a]	Share of Small Farmers in			
		Number of Institutional Loans	Amount of Institutional Loans	Total Farmers	Total Land
	(hectares)		(percent)		
Sub-Saharan Africa					
Middle-income countries					
Kenya	n.a.	n.a.	41	n.a.	n.a.
Asia					
Low-income countries					
Bangladesh	1	73	49	66	24
India					
1974-75	2	56	33	63	21
1980-81	2	61	39	75	26
Pakistan	4	n.a.	23	n.a.	n.a.
Simple average for mid-1970s	...	64.50	41.00	64.50	22.50
Middle-income countries					
Korea, Republic of	1	71	n.a.	68	50
Malaysia	2	36	18	72	48
Taiwan	2	n.a.	73	n.a.	n.a.
Simple average	...	53.50	45.50	70.00	49.00
Latin America and the Caribbean					
Low-income country					
Bolivia	10	5	6	50	n.a.
Middle-income countries					
Brazil	10	15	32	51	n.a.
Chile	10	41	16	50	n.a.
Colombia	10	42	38	77	n.a.
Costa Rica	10	34	18	67	n.a.
Ecuador	30	n.a.	24	n.a.	n.a.
El Salvador	10	85	7	n.a.	n.a.
Honduras	10	91	19	n.a.	n.a.
Mexico	10	15	12	85	n.a.
Peru	10	15	n.a.	92	n.a.
Simple average	...	42.25	20.75	70.33	n.a.

Sources: Donald 1976; India 1971, 1977, 1981; Olin 1975; Rangarajan 1974; and Reserve Bank of India various issues a, various issues b.
[a]Small farmers may own up to the number of hectares indicated.

Functional Structure of RFIs and the RFI System in General

Multifunctional RFIs are defined as those that *directly* and *indirectly* undertake functions such as farm-level loans (both in cash and kind, and short- and longer-term loans for crops and other enterprises), extension, sales of farm inputs, marketing of farm produce, sales of consumer goods, collection of deposits, other borrowings, and loan recovery. Past literature has emphasized improved coordination among RFIs, extension agencies, and other organizations engaged in auxiliary services (FAO 1973, 1974a, 1974b, 1975, 1976). This study also notes two additional mechanisms through which RFIs play their multifunctional role. The higher-level cooperative RFIs—those at the apex and intermediate level—promote financial services to their lower-level constituents for activities such as farm input sales, produce marketing, and consumer goods sales. RFIs that are not cooperatives also promote financial services to their private- and public-sector clients engaged in these activities. In other words, all RFIs do not themselves sell farm inputs and services, but they participate in those activities by making loans and extending other financial services to those engaged directly in those businesses.

For agricultural growth, intermediate inputs (such as seeds and fertilizer), labor, and operating assets (such as wells, pumpsets, and farm implements) are all required and complement each other. Credit makes it possible for farmers to have the inputs they need to realize the full potential of the new technology[10] and hence to repay loans promptly (Deaton 1989; B. M. Desai 1989; Desai and Rao 1978; Desai, Gupta, and Singh 1988). Multifunctional RFIs have the following advantages: (1) they facilitate complementarities between intermediate inputs, labor, and operating assets, enabling farmers to have inputs available when they need them; (2) they encourage diversification of agriculture and development of other economic activities that complement or supplement agriculture; and (3) they promote the noninflationary production and saving linkages of technological change in agriculture, as well as consumption linkages resulting from increased rural incomes; (4) they offer effective alternatives to informal lenders; and (5) through economies of scale, they collect a larger share of loans promptly, hence recycling funds more often, thus increasing their own viability.

Farm-level credit, when extended not only for crop farming but also for dairying and other directly related farm-level economic activities, encourages diversified agriculture, which stabilizes and perhaps increases resource productivity, agricultural production, value added, and net incomes of farmers. In other words, what results is a more rewarding and robust agricultural sector and better loan repayment capacity.

Credit to farmers acts as an impetus to investment in real resources, which must be matched by supplies. Loans to farm input and produce

---

[10]New technology shifts agriculture's total cost function inward and hence leads to lower cost per unit of output.

marketing agencies help increase the availability of such supplies. Through the various types of agricultural credit, RFIs can accomplish two necessary tasks: they can achieve better balance between demand and supply forces and hence are noninflationary, and they can promote backward (BWL) and forward (FWL) linkages among the three directly interdependent subsystems of agriculture shown in the diagram below. The three subsystems are the agricultural production system (APS), the agricultural inputs distribution system (AIS), and the agro-marketing and processing system (AMPS) (B. M. Desai 1989; Desai, Gupta, and Singh 1988; Desai, Gupta, and Tripathi 1989; and Desai and Namboodiri 1991).

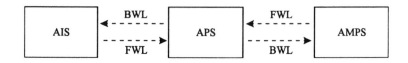

Multifunctional RFIs can be an effective alternative to informal lenders because they undertake a range of functions. In most developing countries, informal private lenders extend loans in kind as well as in cash. That is, they loan seeds, raw materials, grain, and so forth and recover their value through produce or wage labor. In other words, their operations are characterized by horizontal integration of local commodity, land, labor, and credit markets (Asian Productivity Organization 1984, 1985; D. G. R. Belshaw 1988b; H. Belshaw 1959; Bhaduri 1973; Bhattacharya 1978; Braverman and Guash 1986; Dantwala 1966; B. M. Desai 1976, 1980; Donald 1976; FAO 1973, 1974a, 1974b, 1975, 1976; Feder et al. 1989; Firth and Yamey 1964; Hossain 1988; Kato 1984; Mellor 1966; Reserve Bank of India 1945, 1954; Rosen 1975). Under these circumstances, if formal RFIs concentrate on merely providing credit alone, they cannot compete as effectively as informal lenders in integrating rural people, especially the rural poor, into a national financial system. Moreover, rural clients urgently need modern physical inputs and services to improve their land and labor productivity.

Multifunctional RFIs benefit greatly from economies of scale and scope and thereby improve their viability. Such economies result from spreading many common transaction costs among the various functions; mobilizing low-cost deposits, hence lowering interest costs; extending loans that carry lower as well as higher lending rates; improving loan recovery rates, thus being able to recycle funds quicker; and increasing earnings from many nonfinancial activities, including commissions on nonfund-based credit, check-clearing fees, discounts on bills, and income from auxiliary services such as input sales, consumer goods sales, and farm-produce marketing (B. M. Desai 1989; Desai, Gupta, and Singh 1988; Desai, Gupta, and Tripathi 1989; Desai and Namboodiri 1991).

Empirical evidence quantifying each of these advantages does not exist. But deductive reasoning, observations, cross-national comparisons approximated from available literature, and quotations from the literature concerning the experiences of RFIs in some countries form the bases for the information presented here. Cross-national comparisons of RFIs are presented in Table 5 and discussed in detail in Chapter 5. A lengthy compilation of relevant quotations is available from the International Food Policy Research Institute upon request.

Before examining Table 5, however, two overall conclusions of the comprehensive analysis should be discussed. Vertically organized, multifunctional RFIs—widely found in a few countries including Japan, the Republic of Korea, Taiwan, and the United States—have been acclaimed for their success in both agricultural and rural financial market development. They are also found in the People's Republic of China, Egypt, and Syria. Moreover, they are rapidly emerging in all the major Asian developing countries—Bangladesh, India, Indonesia, Pakistan, Malaysia, and Thailand. There are one or two RFIs in some countries in Latin America and the Caribbean (Brazil, Chile, Cuba, and Mexico), in the Near East and Mediterranean Basin (Sudan, Cyprus, and Jordan), and in Sub-Saharan Africa (Tanzania, Togo, Cameroon, and Kenya). But, in most parts of the developing world, RFIs are by and large unifunctional.

In many Asian and some Near East and Mediterranean Basin countries and in the United States, local credit cooperatives undertake a multifunctional role because their regional and national federations make loans to them and assist them in acquiring storage facilities. Such loans and infrastructure enable the local cooperatives to enter into trading in farm inputs, farm produce, and consumer goods in addition to making farm-level production loans. This may also be the case in some parts of Latin America. The role of cooperative credit in India is depicted in Figure 3. Other RFIs in these countries also fill multifunctional roles by providing credit for input business operations and produce-marketing agencies, in addition to other functions.[11] The figure indicates how RFIs in these countries have promoted credit and other services to the three subsystems.

In Table 5, various types of RFIs are divided into unifunctional, semi-multifunctional, and multifunctional operations. Similarly, the RFI systems of countries are divided into these three categories by region and income group.

Unifunctional RFIs largely concentrate on short-term farm-level credit, extension, other borrowings, and loan recovery. Semi-multifunctional RFIs undertake not only these functions, but also some longer-term farm-level credit, input sales, and funds collection. In this classification scheme, all RFIs are not necessarily expected to play a direct multifunctional role. Some may coordinate with input- and produce-marketing agencies or promote financial services to these agencies. Together they

---

[11]These are indeed different from those nonfinancial agencies that merely transfer government funds to farmers in the form of inputs and recover them by purchasing their produce (often without charging interest), which are prevalent in Africa and Latin America, particularly for perishable and semiperishable agricultural commodities that are exported.

Table 5—Proportion of rural financial institutions (RFIs) and country RFI systems that are unifunctional, semi-multifunctional, and multifunctional, by region and income group

Region/Income Group	Number of Countries Covered	Percent of Countries Where Formal RFI System Is			Percent of RFIs That Are		
		Uni-functional	Semi-multifunctional	Multi-functional	Uni-functional	Semi-multifunctional	Multi-functional
Sub-Saharan Africa							
Low-income countries	18	89	11	0	64	36	0
Middle-income countries	14	43	57	0	58	40	2
Asia							
Low-income countries	9	11	78	11	23	71	6
Middle-income countries	5	0	60	40	17	47	36
	(2)	(0)	(0)	(100)	(0)	(9)	(91)
	[3]	[0]	[100]	[0]	[26]	[69]	[5]
High-income country	1	0	0	100	0	12	88
Near East and Mediterranean Basin							
Low-income countries	2	0	100	0	12	88	0
Middle-income countries	8	0	62	38	39	44	17
High-income countries	1	0	100	0	60	40	0
North America							
High-income country	1	0	0	100	20	40	40
Latin America and the Caribbean							
Low-income countries	3	33	67	0	36	55	9
Middle-income countries	27	19	81	0	32	68	0

Sources: Asian Productivity Organization 1984, 1985, 1988; Brake et al. 1971, Philippines, Bureau of Cooperatives Development 1979; Thailand Cooperatives Promotion Department 1979; B. M. Desai 1986b, 1989; Desai, Gupta, and Singh 1988; Desai and Namboodiri 1991; Donald 1976; Egaitsu 1988b; FAO 1973, 1974a, 1974b, 1975, 1976; Hossain 1988; Hussi and Abbott 1975; Hyun, Adams, and Hushak 1979; Jodha 1974; C. Y. Lee 1983; D. H. Lee 1984; Lee, Bohlje, and Nelson 1980; Machima 1976; Matsuhiro 1988; Meyer, Baker, and Onchon 1979; Mohnan 1986; Murray 1961; NENARCA 1987; Rana 1973; Korea, Republic of, NACF various years; Singh 1970; Tashiro 1984; Central Union of Agricultural Cooperatives 1971, 1980a, 1980b; and Norinchukin Bank 1985.

Notes: Numbers in parentheses are for Taiwan and the Republic of Korea combined. Numbers in brackets are for Malaysia, the Philippines, and Thailand combined. Income groups of countries are based on real national income.

37

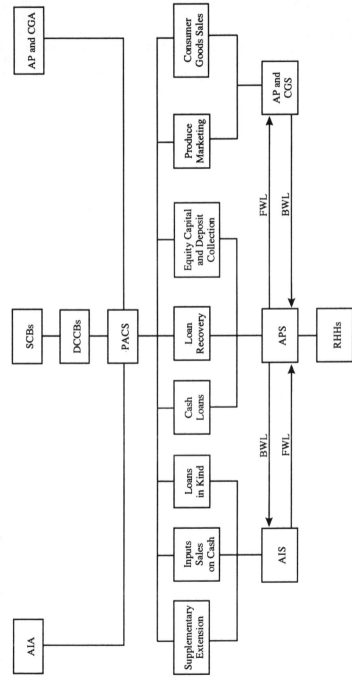

Figure 3—Stylized organizational frame of the multifunctional role of cooperative credit institutions in India

Notes: AIA, agricultural inputs agencies; AP and CGA, agricultural produce and consumer goods agencies; SCBs, state cooperative banks; DCCBs, district central cooperative banks; PACS, primary agricultural cooperative credit societies; AIS, agricultural inputs distribution subsystem; APS, agricultural production subsystem; AP and CGS, agricultural produce and consumer goods subsystem; RHHs, rural households; BWL, backward linkage; FWL, forward linkage.

are integrated to form a multifunctional RFI system in order to improve the rate of return on investments by farmers.

From Table 5 it is clear that larger proportions of RFIs in higher income countries in Asia and North America are multifunctional and semi-multifunctional. Surprisingly, Asian LICs stand next to these countries in this regard, followed by Asian MICs, other than Taiwan and the Republic of Korea. African MICs and LICs have few if any multifunctional RFIs. The Near East and Mediterranean Basin appears to have RFIs with better functional structures than Latin America and the Caribbean.

5

Transaction Costs, Profitability, Economies of Scale, and Their Effects on Development

Transaction costs, defined later in this chapter, are largely under the control of rural financial institutions. Subsequent chapters show that the level of interest rates influences the level of investment in rural development. Since transaction costs help determine interest rates, either directly through competitive market forces or through their influence on the administrative setting of lending rates, it is important to measure them and to understand what determines them. A substantial amount of recent literature argues that because transaction costs in low-income countries are high and rising, RFIs are generally not profitable, and they have contributed little or even negatively to agricultural development (Adams and Kato 1978; Ahmed and Adams 1987; Cuevas 1987a; Von Pischke, Adams, and Donald 1983). Analysis in this chapter is organized around the following information:

- Importance of the issue of the transaction costs involved in lending to farmers vis-à-vis all other activities of RFIs;
- Definitions and concepts regarding these costs and their relation to the viability of RFIs;
- Cross-national comparison of transaction costs on a comparable basis; and
- Transaction costs of selected RFIs, scale relationships, and viability, and the developmental accomplishments of RFIs in various countries.

Importance of Considering Transaction Costs for All Activities of RFIs

Some critics of past agricultural credit policy have exclusively dealt with the transaction costs involved when RFIs lend to farmers (Ahmed and Adams 1987; Cuevas 1987a, 1987b; Cuevas and Graham 1984; Gadgil 1986; Gheen 1976; Meyer and Srinivasan 1987; Meyer, Baker, and Onchon 1979; Nyanin 1982; Saito and Villanueva 1981; Srinivasan and Meyer 1986). There are severe limitations to this approach.

First, this approach is inconsistent with policy concerns about viability and the transaction costs of an institution rather than consideration of a single product, such as lending.[12] Second, it assumes that all transaction costs can be attributed to lending, which cannot be done without borrowing from somewhere. Third, it does not recognize that products of financial institutions are multiple and joint. Examples of multiple products include different types of loans, deposits, share capital, and nonfund-based credit. Examples of joint products are increased lending related to increased deposits, refinancing provided only after lending, and borrowing by RFIs from a central financing agency of their own funds or some proportion of their loan recoveries or their performance in deposit mobilization. Fourth, transaction costs are common to all these activities and hence their allocation to various activities is arbitrary and difficult.[13] Fifth, some of the studies that have the above limitations define average transaction costs as a percentage of loans made to farmers or the number of accounts of farmer loans, while others consider this cost as a percentage of outstanding balances of farmer loans. Finally, estimation of these costs and the scale economies in them are highly sensitive to the definition of output of an RFI. Estimated parameters of econometric cost functions are also characterized by this weakness. These studies therefore cannot be compared. As many as 18 out of 22 have these limitations.

An obvious conclusion is that the issue of transaction costs of institutional lenders must be conceptualized and measured for all activities of RFIs, rather than for only one activity such as making farm loans or collecting deposits. Hence, these costs and their measures in units or percentages must be properly specified.

Definitions and Concepts of Transaction Costs and Viability of RFIs

Transaction costs are of two types: administrative costs and the cost of bad debts. The former is addressed more comprehensively, though it does not underplay the importance of the latter. However, the high shares of overdue loans and the implied bad debts suggested in some studies grossly overstate the problem. This is because the measure of loan delinquency and the implication that the supply of credit is restrained as a result of unpaid loans does not allow for such factors as loans repaid after a reasonable period past the maturity date, age of overdues, unsatisfactory loan appraisal and recovery policies and procedures, and demands for loans from borrowers with genuine delinquency

---

[12]These critics also share the view that the viability of an RFI is the basic issue. According to analysis of most of the other issues by these critics, they consider a financial intermediary as a unit of analysis of conceptualization (Adams and Kato 1978; Cuevas 1984; Von Pischke, Adams, and Donald 1983).

[13]This is also true for traditional moneylenders who also undertake nonlending activities such as trading and hiring labor.

or from new borrowers. Moreover, a view prevails that overdue loans may be considered transfers and not costs of resources employed. But loan delinquency and the associated costs of bad debts must not be ignored because they can adversely affect the long-run viability of the RFIs. The extent of these costs could not be estimated for this study, however, because the required data were not available. Therefore it is urgent that RFIs improve their data base on delinquent loans.

The first type of transaction costs—administrative or managerial— usually includes costs of personnel, office space, postage, stationery, printing, travel, audits, training, and related maintenance costs. To make these costs comparable across RFIs within a country or over various countries, they must be defined in unit or percentage terms, that is, in unit (or average) transaction costs. This, in turn, raises a question about how the total transaction costs should be divided: What should be the definition of output of RFIs? The normal convention is to express these costs as a percentage of loanable resources—that is, on the liabilities side of the balance sheet of any RFI (Revell 1980; Varde and Singh 1982, 1983; Verghese 1983). This implies that loanable funds are an output of every RFI, but this is unsatisfactory. Following the discussion in the preceding section, output of an RFI should be defined as all assets plus all liabilities for two reasons. First, asset items such as loans and investments are obviously the outputs of an RFI. And second, liabilities are also an output because of the joint nature of assets and liabilities of an institution such as a financial intermediary. Unit transaction costs are, therefore, defined as total transaction costs as a percentage of all liabilities plus assets, excluding contra items such as bills, drafts of other banks, and guarantees. Similar approaches are found in Cuevas 1984; B. M. Desai 1986b; Desai, Gupta, and Tripathi 1989; Desai and Namboodiri 1991; Virmani 1984. This approach is different from that used in accounting and financial management literature, which defines average transaction costs as a percentage of liabilities. But this can be derived from the estimate based on the approach used in this study by simply doubling the cost, since liabilities equal assets.

After critically but constructively reviewing the literature, the concept of profitability of RFIs needs to be discussed.[14] For this, it is important to recognize that any financial institution has financial costs besides the transaction costs required for its business. These costs, plus the transaction costs, make up the total costs. To measure the viability of a financial institution, total costs must be subtracted from the RFI's interest revenue from all loans plus noninterest revenue, and not just from interest revenue from farm loans.

These costs and revenues must be in unit terms. The basic unit that follows from the earlier discussion of definitions of output is derived from all assets plus all liabilities, excluding contra items. According to this definition, like transaction costs, financial costs and gross revenue

---

[14]This discussion is restricted to the concept of viability in an explicit sense, that is, without considering the cost of bad debts, because the available literature does not deal with this subject nor does it provide the data required.

must be measured in unit or percentage terms, which would then express average financial costs and average gross revenue. The difference between average gross revenue and average financial costs can be termed average gross margin. If gross margin is higher than average transaction costs, the RFI is viable; if average gross margin is lower than average transaction costs, the RFI is not viable; and if average gross margin and average transaction costs are the same, the RFI is breaking even. However, viability measured in this way does not consider the cost of bad and doubtful debts. It must be emphasized again that conceptualization of unit transaction costs, unit financial costs, and unit gross margin is most appropriate to understanding one of the goals of an RFI, namely, its viability.[15] This forms the basis for analyzing the subsequent sections.

Cross-National Comparison of Unit Transaction Costs

Table 6 gives the transaction costs for RFIs in selected LICs and MICs in the different geographical regions in the mid-1970s. Asian LICs have lower unit transaction costs (2.4 percent) than some Asian MICs (the Philippines and Thailand) (3.3 percent), African MICs (3.1 percent), and Latin American and Caribbean MICs (2.8 percent). This may be because more RFIs in Asian LICs are multifunctional.

Average transaction costs vary, though the variation within a group of countries with different per capita income levels is not significant. The exceptions seem to be African and Latin American and Caribbean MICs, perhaps because in most Asian countries RFIs are likely to be vertically and horizontally integrated, and these countries have better basic infrastructural facilities. It may also be because many RFIs in Asia are older than those in other regions.

Nevertheless, average transaction costs of institutional lenders are about 2-3 percent for most of the countries, irrespective of whether the figure is an average or a median, though the median is a little lower than or equal to the average in all regions except Latin America and the Caribbean. In this case, the median unit transaction cost is 3.0 percent as opposed to an average unit transaction cost of 2.8 percent.

The mean value (simple average) of unit transaction costs is lowest in the Asian MICs, the Republic of Korea and Taiwan (1.3 percent), followed by the Near East and Mediterranean MICs (1.7 percent), Asian LICs (2.4 percent), Latin American and Caribbean MICs (2.8 percent), African MICs (3.1 percent), and Asian MICs consisting of the Philippines and Thailand (3.3 percent). This suggests that institutional lenders have been relatively more successful in keeping their transaction costs lower in some Asian MICs and LICs and in the Near East and Mediter-

---

[15]Viability so measured may indicate that an entity is not viable at a given point in time, but that does not imply that it will always remain so. It may have the potential to be viable in the future through expansion of its size, the multifunctional role, and so on.

Table 6—Unit transaction costs of selected institutional lenders, by region and country, mid-1970s

Region/Country	Type of Institution	Unit Transaction Cost[a]
		(percent)
Sub-Saharan Africa		
Middle-income countries		
Côte d'Ivoire	Agricultural Development Bank[b]	5.00
Ghana	Caisse National de Crédit Agricole[b]	4.50
Kenya	Agricultural Finance Corporation[bc]	1.50
Senegal	Bank for National Development[b]	1.50
Simple average		3.13
		(3.00)
Asia		
Low-income countries		
Bangladesh	Kotwali Thane Central Cooperative Association[d]	5.00
	Bangladesh Krishi Bank[b]	1.50
India	Land Development Bank (Cooperative)[cd]	1.50
Pakistan	Agricultural Development Bank[bc]	1.50
Simple average		2.37
		(1.50)
Middle-income countries		
Taiwan	Farmers' Associations[d]	1.25
	Cooperative Banks[d]	1.25
	Land Banks[d]	0.75
Korea, Republic of	National Agricultural Cooperative Federation[d]	2.00
Philippines	Rural banks (private)[c]	2.50
Thailand	Bank for Agriculture and Agricultural Cooperatives[b]	4.00
Simple average for Taiwan and Korea		1.31 (1.25)
Simple average for the Philippines and Thailand		3.25 (3.25)
Near East and Mediterranean Basin		
Middle-income countries		
Jordan	Agricultural Credit Corporation[bc]	1.50
Lebanon	Lebanese Credit Bank for Agricultural and Industrial Development[b]	1.50
Morocco	Caisse National de Crédit Agricole[bc]	1.50
Turkey	Supervised Credit Programme[e]	1.00
	Turkish Republican Agricultural Bank[b]	3.00
Simple average		1.70
		(1.50)
Latin America and Caribbean		
Middle-income countries		
Colombia	Instituto Colombiano de la Reforme Agrarine[e]	3.50
Costa Rica	Banco Nacional de Costa Rica[b]	1.50
Simple average		2.80
		(3.00)

Sources: Saito and Villanueva 1981; World Bank 1973.
Note: Numbers in parentheses are medians.
[a]Unit transaction costs are defined as noninterest transaction and administrative costs as a percentage of all assets plus all liabilities (resources). These costs are for an institution rather than for any one of its activities.
[b]Government-sponsored RFI.
[c]Institutions involved in a World Bank project.
[d]Cooperative.
[e]Government project.

ranean MICs than in either African or Latin American and Caribbean MICs. The reasons for this are perhaps the same as those discussed above.

The average transaction cost for the majority of government-sponsored banks (8 out of 13) and cooperatives (5 out of 6) are lower than those for government projects (2 out of 4) and private rural banks. For government-sponsored banks and cooperatives, it ranges from 0.8 to 2.0 percent, while for government projects and private rural banks, it varies from 2.5 to 5.5 percent.

The Asian MICs consisting of Taiwan and the Republic of Korea, where the RFI systems are both vertically and horizontally integrated, have unit transaction costs of barely 1.3 percent. This suggests that multifunctional RFIs have the potential to reduce their average transaction costs significantly. Multifunctional RFIs result not only from autonomous forces of development but also from deliberate policies undertaken to promote financial services for farmers and for projects of other agricultural support institutions.

Country Case Studies of Selected RFIs

Thirteen case studies are analyzed in this study—two in Bangladesh, four in India, three each in Thailand and the Republic of Korea, and one in Sudan. The two case studies in Bangladesh cover 4 RFIs. The four in India deal with 13 RFIs, the three in Thailand and the Republic of Korea cover 3 each, and the one in Sudan covers 2. The forms of organization of these 28 RFIs are state-sponsored agricultural or rural banks, nationalized commercial banks, and cooperative banks or their constituents at the grassroots level.

Grameen Bank, Bangladesh

The Grameen Bank, established by the government in 1983 to extend credit to the rural poor, has achieved its twin objectives of economic development and poverty alleviation and has emerged as a viable financial institution (Hossain 1988). This is largely because it is multifunctional and offers an effective alternative to informal lenders—an achievement that would not have been possible without visionary leadership and decentralized organizational and management systems. A strategy to reduce administrative costs by reaping further scale economies would improve its viability even more. Enlarging the scale of operations and changing its composition is more important than upward revisions in lending or borrowing rates. Scale economies can be enhanced by expanding coverage of clients with small-scale loans or deposits on an individual basis. This can also be accomplished by enlarging the scope of loans to include working capital credit for livestock farming.

The Grameen Bank originated from a small action research project undertaken in 1976. Seventy-five percent of its paid-up capital is now owned by the bank's shareholders—its borrowers—and 25 percent by the government. During the period 1984-86, the bank funded its operations largely by borrowing from the Bangladesh Bank (9-41 percent), from the International Fund for Agricultural Development (IFAD) (33-35 percent), and from the Netherlands (5-9 percent). Another small but significant source of funds has been the group fund created by the borrower shareholders (7-9 percent) during the same period.

As a result of expansion of the bank, a decentralization of administration has taken place, with responsibilities and decisionmaking powers vested in a cadre of mid-level officials who are strongly motivated by the bank's founder and managing director.

By early 1987, the bank had 298 branches. These covered 25 percent of the target-group households in two districts and 8 percent in the remaining three districts that form the area of operations of the bank.

Nearly 96 percent of its loans have been advanced to households owning less than 0.2 hectare. These loans are extended at an annual interest rate of 16 percent. The bank has a diversified loan portfolio that consists not only of farm-level loans but also loans to local agroprocessing and trading operations. The major enterprises financed are crop farms, milch cows, paddy and rice trade, seasonal crop trade, cattle and goat trade, handloom weaving, clothing trade, and grocery and other shops. The bank has encouraged investment, employment, and occupational diversification, in addition to increasing incomes and lowering poverty among the rural poor. The loan recovery performance is excellent because supervision is intensive due to high expenditures on administration and because the rate of return on activities financed is high; many of these loans generate an almost continuous flow of income to the borrowers.

As a whole, the average transaction costs of the Grameen Bank were about 3 percent during 1984-86 (Table 7). Margins exceeded transaction costs during the period. Both average and marginal transaction costs increased in 1985 and again in 1987. But unit as well as marginal financial or interest costs first increased and then declined significantly. Unit revenue from interest earnings on loans and other earnings first increased and then declined.

Considering the difference between unit revenue and unit financial costs, unit gross margin first increased and then remained more or less constant. But, unit net margin, which is the difference between unit gross margin and unit transaction costs, declined, the fall being substantial in 1985 and significant in 1986.

The Grameen Bank had scale diseconomies in transaction costs but scale economies in financial costs (Table 8). The scale diseconomies in transaction costs are perhaps the result of rapid expansion and the low volume typical of new branches. The scale economies in financial costs, however, were mainly the result of the bank's strategy of borrowing low-cost funds (from IFAD). Had the bank used these funds to extend loans instead of to invest in low-earning deposits with other agencies, it would have improved its viability and used its administrative resources more fully to reap scale economies in transaction costs. This would also have resulted from investment in assets with higher earnings, such as loans.

This is not to undermine the significant achievement of the bank in achieving viability through a positive though small unit net margin, a higher loan collection rate, and some voluntary mobilization of deposits.

Table 7—Costs and viability of the Grameen Bank, Bangladesh, 1984-86

Variable in Real Terms[a]	Three-Year Average	1984	1985	1986
	(percent)			
Unit transaction costs[b]	2.98	1.95	3.21	3.27
Unit financial costs[b]	2.10	2.12	2.71	1.72
Unit revenue[b]	5.27	4.78	6.02	5.01
Unit gross margin[b] (Row 3 minus Row 2)	3.17	2.66	3.31	3.29
Unit net margin[b] (Row 4 minus Row 1)	0.19	0.71	0.10	0.02
Marginal transaction costs[c]	4.91	4.40	10.51	16.17
Marginal financial costs[c]	1.53	2.14	3.90	3.73

Source: Hossain 1988.
[a]Real terms are derived by applying the agricultural GDP deflator with a base year of 1972/73.
[b]Unit costs are computed as a percentage of all assets plus all liabilities.
[c]Marginal costs are derived from the estimated cost functions, the results of which are reported in Table 8.

It should be emphasized, however, that the Grameen Bank could have reaped scale economies in its transaction costs. That this is possible is clearly shown in Table 9, where the branches of the Grameen Bank reach a low point in unit and marginal transaction costs when they are about three years old and reap scale economies in these costs as they grow in experience.

Table 8—Estimated parameters of double-log cost functions for the Grameen Bank, Bangladesh

Dependent Variable in Real Terms	Coefficients Related to		$\bar{R}^2$	Scale Parameter	Number of Observations
	Constant	Assets Plus Liabilities in Real Terms			
Transaction costs	−7.035	1.648 (4.449)[a]	0.904	1.65[b]	3
Financial or interest costs	−2.368	0.722 (1.418)[c]	0.330	0.72[d]	3

Notes: Figures in parentheses are t-values.
[a]Significant at 20 percent.
[b]Significantly greater than 1. This implies that when the scale of operations increases by 1 percent, transaction costs increase by more than 1 percent, which suggests diseconomies of scale in these costs.
[c]Significant at 40 percent
[d]Significantly less than 1. This implies that when the scale of operations increases by 1 percent, financial costs increase by less than 1 percent, which suggests economies of scale in these costs.

Table 9—Transaction costs of branches of the Grameen Bank, Bangladesh, 1984-85

Age of Branch	Unit Transaction Costs[a]	Marginal Transaction Costs[b]
	(percent)	
Up to 6 months	19.56	9.39
6 months-1 year	12.92	5.56
1.0-1.5 years	6.79	2.72
1.5-2.0 years	5.34	2.14
2.0-2.5 years	4.48	1.75
2.5-3.0 years	4.31	1.68
More than 3 years	4.51	1.76
Average	5.41	2.16

Source: Hossain 1988.
[a]These are computed as a percentage of loans outstanding plus deposit balances.
[b]These are derived from the estimated log-log inverse cost function, the results of which are given in Table 10.

In Table 10, the scale parameter of 0.40 indicates that when the volume of business of a branch increases by 100 percent, the transaction costs increase by only 40 percent. This suggests that the viability of a branch could be improved by taking advantage of scale economies in transaction costs instead of raising interest rates on loans or administratively improving interest spreads or margins, hence benefiting the poor who are the main clients of the bank. Indeed, these branches did not suffer at all from scale diseconomies and continued to enjoy scale economies in these costs even beyond 5.5 million taka (Figure 4).

Table 10—Estimated parameters of the log-log inverse transaction cost function for branches of the Grameen Bank, Bangladesh

		Coefficients Related to				
Dependent Variable	Con- stant	Loans Outstanding and Deposit Balances	Inverse of Loans Outstanding and Deposit Balances	$\bar{R}^2$	Scale Param- eter	Number of Obser- vations
Transaction costs	−2.498	0.386[a] (9.399)	−20.112 (−0.801)[c]	0.995	0.40[b]	7

Notes: Figures in parentheses are t-values.
[a]Significant at 1 percent.
[b]Significantly less than 1, implying economies of scale.
[c]Significant at 50 percent.

48

**Figure 4—Behavior of scale economies in transaction costs
of sample branches of the Grameen Bank,
Bangladesh, 1984-85**

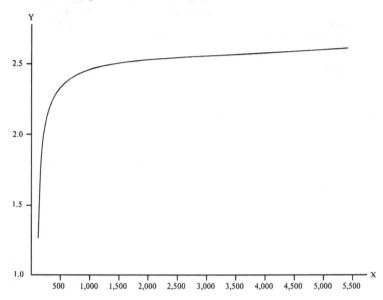

Source: Derived from Table 10.
Notes: Y = Reciprocal of elasticity of transaction costs with respect to volume of business.
        X = Volume of business (loans plus deposit balances in Tk 1,000).

Sonali Bank, Bangladesh

Sonali Bank, one of six nationalized commercial banks in Bangladesh, earned a positive unit net margin and hence was viable during 1976-80 (Virmani 1984). However, it did not take full advantage of scale economies in its administrative or transaction costs. These costs could plausibly have been reduced by expanding its volume of operations, which are multifunctional. The bank's rural branches have enjoyed scale economies in transaction costs and appear to have potential for diversifying their lending and nonlending operations. During the period 1976-80, the ratio of rural to urban branches continuously increased:

Year	Ratio of Rural to Urban Branches
1976	1.25
1977	1.58
1978	1.63
1979	2.01
1980	2.09

The Sonali Bank's unit net margin is underestimated because unit gross margin is computed as a simple average of the interest spread on loans to the farm sector alone, although the bank serves all sectors. Also the unit net margin does not include revenues such as commissions, bank guarantees, and check-clearing fees, which are earnings from non-fund-based products that also entail a part of the same transaction costs.

Sonali Bank's unit and incremental transaction costs varied, but only marginally (Table 11). Average unit transaction costs were only 1.7 percent during 1976-80. The unit gross margin averaged 3.4 percent, which leaves a unit net margin of 1.7 percent after unit transaction costs are subtracted.

The Sonali Bank neither suffered from scale diseconomies nor enjoyed scale economies in these costs (Table 12). This suggests that the bank could realize further economies of scale and improve its unit net margin by expanding its volume of operations, especially in rural areas, for two reasons. First, the bank has significantly expanded its rural branch network, as shown in the table on the previous page. And second, rural branches are also viable and have enjoyed scale economies in their transaction costs (Tables 13 and 14). Unit transaction costs of these branches declined significantly with the increase in the volume of their business. Moreover, the low point in unit transaction costs of these branches comes when their scale of operations reaches at least Tk 3 million. In other words, these branches can spread their common and joint costs of transaction more once their operations reach this particular value. Not only would this make possible greater scale economies, but it would also improve the unit net margin, as is the case for branches

Table 11—Unit and marginal transaction costs and viability of the Sonali Bank, Bangladesh, 1976-80

Variable in Real Terms[a]	Five-Year Average	1976	1977	1978	1979	1980
Unit transaction costs[b]	1.65	1.75	1.49	1.74	1.58	1.69
Unit gross margin[c]	3.40	3.40	3.40	3.40	3.40	3.40
Unit net margin[d]	1.75	1.65	1.91	1.66	1.82	1.71
Marginal transaction costs[e]	1.63	1.73	1.48	1.72	1.59	1.67

Source: Virmani 1984.

[a] Real terms are derived by applying the agricultural GDP deflator to a base year of 1972/73.

[b] Computed as a percent of loans outstanding plus deposit balances.

[c] Computed as the difference between the farm lending rate and the simple average rate for deposits and refinances divided by 2. These rates are from Agabin 1988a, 6. Weighted averages could not be used because data were not available. For the same reason, unit revenues from noninterest earnings (such as commissions, bank fees, and so forth) could not be used and hence the unit gross margin is underestimated.

[d] Unit gross margin minus unit transaction costs.

[e] Derived from the estimated double-log function, the results of which are reported in Table 12.

Table 12—Estimated parameters of the double-log transaction cost function for the Sonali Bank, Bangladesh

Dependent Variable in Real Terms	Constant	Coefficients Related to Assets Plus Liabilities in Real Terms	$\bar{R}^2$	Scale Parameter	Number of Observations
Transaction costs	-4.072	0.991[a] (7.134)	0.926	0.99[b]	5

Notes: Figures in parentheses are t-values.
[a]Significant at 1 percent.
[b]Statistically not significantly different from 1, suggesting that scale economies have been fully realized.

with larger scales of operations (see the last column in row 3 in Table 13). Even this unit net margin is underestimated because it is based on a simple average of the interest spread for loans to the farm sector only. As is the case for the Sonali Bank as a whole, earnings from loans to agriculture support agencies and from nonfund-based product lines are not considered.

The net margin of any RFI can be improved either by improving the interest spread or by reaping economies of scale in transaction costs by enlarging the scale and scope of operations. These findings suggest that it is possible to improve the net margin of the Sonali Bank through the second alternative. This is also consistent with the finding that the response to interest rates of rural demand for loans is highly elastic and the supply of deposits is feeble in low-income countries, as will be shown in subsequent chapters on these topics.

Table 13—Unit and marginal transaction costs and viability of 10 rural branches of the Sonali Bank, Bangladesh

Variable	Average	Size Groups 1	2	3
Unit transaction costs[a]	5.32	6.94	4.80	4.68
Unit gross margin[b]	5.36	5.36	5.36	5.36
Unit net margin[c]	0.04	-0.58	0.56	0.68
Marginal transaction costs[d]	3.89	2.97	3.73	4.13

Source: Virmani 1984.
[a]Computed as a percentage of loans outstanding plus deposit balances.
[b]Computed as the difference between the lending rate and the average cost of deposits divided by 2. These data are from Agabin 1988a, 6, 28.
[c]Unit gross margin minus unit transaction costs.
[d]Derived from the estimated log-log-inverse function, the results of which are reported in Table 14.

Table 14—Estimated parameters of the log-log inverse transaction cost function for branches of the Sonali Bank, Bangladesh

| Dependent Variable | Con-stant | Coefficients Related to | | $\bar{R}^2$ | Scale Param-eter | Number of Obser-vatons |
		Loans Outstanding and Deposit Balances	Inverse of Loans Outstanding and Deposit Balances			
Transaction costs	−3.915	1.075[a] (6.712)	820.13[a] (4.269)	0.732	0.73[b]	8

Notes: Figures in parentheses are t-values.
[a]Significant at 1 percent.
[b]Statistically significant at less than 1, suggesting scale economies are possible.

Regional Rural Banks (RRBs), India

The RRBs of India have to some extent diversified their operations in a manner similar to the Grameen Bank (Varde and Singh 1982). A sample of 40 RRBs drawn from different states were viable in both 1978 and 1980 (Table 15); indeed, their viability, on average, improved between the two years. In 1978, the RRBs as a whole had much lower unit financial costs than the commercial banks because they had access to low-cost government financing, but their unit transaction costs were higher because RRBs are much younger institutions than commercial banks, with high start-up costs. In 1978, the unit net margin of the RRBs was lower than that of the commercial banks, but similar information is not available for 1980 for commercial banks.

More important, over the two years, the RRBs, on average, improved their unit net margins. This finding holds for a sample of 40 RRBs taken together as well as for selected RRBs in all regions, although the northern RRBs had negative but improving net margins largely due to an increase in unit financial costs rather than unit transaction costs. Over the two years, an average RRB in all four regions decreased its unit transaction costs.

In all four regions, the unit transaction costs in 1980 were lower than in 1978, as expected, but this was the case for unit financial costs only in the eastern region, where these banks may have had greater access to low-cost funds from depositors, refinancing agencies,[16] or

[16]These refinancing agencies included the Reserve Bank of India (RBI), Agricultural Refinance and Development Corporation (ARDC), and the sponsoring commercial banks. ARDC and the rural credit department of the RBI were merged in the early 1980s to create one national-level refinancing institution called the National Bank for Agriculture and Rural Development (NABARD) to extend both refinancing and rural finance planning facilities to the field-level RFIs.

Table 15—Unit transaction costs, unit interest costs, and unit net margin of the regional rural banks and commercial banks, India, 1978 and 1980

Banks/Region	Unit Transaction Costs[a]		Unit Interest Costs[a]		Unit Net Margin[a]	
	1978	1980	1978	1980	1978	1980
	(percent)					
Commercial banks						
All India	1.28	n.a.	2.79	n.a.	0.07	n.a.
Regional rural banks						
All India	1.70	1.55	1.72	2.32	0.03	0.18
Northern areas	2.14	1.57	1.68	2.27	−0.28	−0.06
Southern areas	1.65	1.52	1.97	2.35	0.23	0.32
Eastern areas	1.98	1.64	2.20	1.72	−0.11	0.20
Central areas	1.80	1.48	1.93	2.55	−0.03	0.12

Source: Varde and Singh 1982.
Notes: n.a. is not available.
Northern areas consist of 5 regional rural banks in Rajasthan and Haryana.
Southern areas consist of 10 regional rural banks in Tamil Nadu, Karnataka, Kerala, and Andhra Pradesh.
Eastern areas consist of 15 regional rural banks in the states of Bihar, Orissa, West Bengal, Tripura, and Assam.
Central areas consist of 10 regional rural banks in Uttar Pradesh and Madhya Pradesh.
[a]Computed as a percentage of all assets plus all liabilities.

both. The sample RRBs had, on average, positive net margins in the southern region in both years, which was only true in 1980 in the eastern and central regions. The result for the northern region may largely be attributed to the fact that Rajasthan, a highly drought-prone semi-arid and arid region, is included as a part of the northern region. Finally, the unit net margin was highest in the south.

Primary Agricultural Cooperative Credit Societies (PACS), India

One of the two PACS studied is multifunctional; the other is not (Desai, Gupta, and Singh 1988). For the multifunctional PACS, unit transaction costs are lower, profitability is higher, and there is no loan delinquency. Farmers under the purview of the multifunctional PACS have larger investments; optimal allocation of resources; better technology; and higher productivity, rates of return, and incomes. This remarkable performance results from better leadership and larger availability of loanable funds for farm-level loans and input distribution businesses.

The two selected primary credit societies form about 10 percent of the sample in Malpur, a backward *taluka* in Sabarkantha District of Gujarat. Both of these PACS are located in the same agroclimatic area with similar infrastructure facilities. One of these PACS is the Aniyorkampa Group Service Cooperative Society (AK PACS), established in February 1979. The other, the Mevda Group Service Cooperative Society (MD

PACS) was established in March 1959. AK PACS serves four villages, MD PACS seven villages. Each has a full-time paid secretary who is assisted by a junior staff member. However, these personnel are supervised by an elected managing committee that is distinctly superior in the AK PACS. Both PACS are vertically aligned with the District Central Cooperative Bank, which itself is a constituent of a state-level cooperative bank.

Based on criteria taking into account the multifunctional role, the impact on the members, and the institution, the AK PACS was more successful than the MD PACS. The AK PACS reached a larger proportion of rural households (63 percent versus 56 percent for membership, and 48 versus 36 percent for borrowing membership). It had a larger share of deposits to loanable resources (13 versus 0 percent); and a larger share of loanable resources in total resources (a debt-equity ratio of 88:14 versus 78:22). It loaned a larger average amount per member (Rs 9,237 versus Rs 2,535 in outstanding loans, and Rs 10,361 versus Rs 1,116 in new loans made), both in short- and long-term loans (a ratio of 60:10 versus 78:22), and a higher share of loans in kind in short-term loans (68 versus 60 percent). It had a larger volume of nonfinancial operations (Rs 1,011 versus Rs 618) and higher concentration on those operations (such as input distribution),[17] which provided greater revenue-earning opportunities to the organization and to its members (the share of such operations being 57 percent versus 33 percent). AK PACS' loan overdues were much lower (delinquency rate was 0.005 versus 44.95 percent). Average transaction costs were lower (0.33 versus 2.10 percent), as well as total costs (transaction plus financial costs of 4.08 versus 7.00 percent), profitability was higher (a profit-to-equity ratio of +18.76 versus –35.35 percent), and the dividend rate was higher (9 versus 0 percent). Finally, farmers under the purview of AK PACS spent more on resources (Rs 5,314 versus Rs 3,258 per hectare), allocated resources better (the extent of suboptimality in the use of modern inputs was 39 versus 60 percent), used technology better (their HYV adoption rate was 34 versus 10 percent and their share of modern input use was 70 versus 42 percent), had more income per hectare (Rs 3,741 versus Rs 3,288), and had a higher rate of return to family capital, labor, and land (27 versus 18 percent).

Among the factors responsible for these accomplishments, four are most prominent. First, leaders of the AK PACS are both enlightened and knowledgeable about the types of operations the organization should undertake to mutually benefit the members and the organization on a sustained basis. Second, the upper-level federal organization made more loanable resources available, including marketing credit, enabling AK PAKS to undertake loans to input-distribution businesses. Third, AK PAKS had larger storage facilities, which made it possible to undertake

---

[17]The nonfinancial operations of the MD PACS were inefficient as a result of organizational arrangements that required MD PACS to obtain inputs from subwholesalers on an informal and indirect basis and in smaller quantities because marketing credit and godown facilities were inadequate.

input distribution. And fourth, members of the managing committee as well as the general membership were committed to their organization's interests.

Nationalized Commercial Banks, India

This case study, drawn from Gothoskar 1989, shows that these banks have penetrated the rural financial market in a major way by expanding branch networks in many remote, unbanked areas. This has improved the mobilization of deposits in rural areas and their share of loans. These banks are vertically organized and are largely multifunctional, serving not only farmers but also support institutions for agricultural development, small-scale industries, trade, and transport. Most of the rural branches in a sample were viable and had achieved economies of scale in transaction costs once their volume of business expanded beyond Rs 1 million.

In 1949, only 16 percent—700 out of 4,263 branches—of commercial banks were in rural areas with populations less than 10,000. Twenty years later, their share had increased to 22 percent, but the share of rural areas in deposits mobilized and loans made remained at 2-3 percent. In July 1969, 14 major commercial banks were nationalized. By 1975, the share of rural branches in the total increased to 27.5 percent, by 1980 to 40 percent, and by 1985 to 54 percent. By 1980, as a result of this expansion in rural branches, the share of commercial banks in loans had increased to 8 percent, and their share in deposits collected had risen to 10.5 percent. And by 1985, the corresponding percentages were 21 and 20 percent. The credit-deposit ratio of rural branches was just about 0.50 by June 1980, increasing to 0.63 in another five years. The increase in deposits during 1980-85 was highest for rural branches, followed by semiurban branches (those with centers of populations of 10,000 to 50,000), urban, and then metropolitan branches of similar age (Table 16).

Three broad types of deposits are mobilized: current, savings, and fixed deposits with maturity periods ranging from 50 days to 5 years. During 1980-85, there was a marginal change in the interest rate offered by these banks on deposits. Current deposits carry no interest rate because they are held briefly for transaction purposes. During 1980-85 increments in loans were allocated to agriculture (18.1 percent), industry (38.5 percent), trade and transport (29.1 percent), and others (14.3 percent). In 1985, rural branches made nearly 50 percent of their loans to agriculture, while semiurban branches made about 33 percent, urban branches 15 percent, and major metropolitan branches 2 percent to agriculture. Industrial loans were the second most important loans in both rural and semiurban branches, while trade and transport claimed the third position.

Analysis of cross-sectional data of a large sample of mostly rural branches shows that they were viable in the mid-1980s (Table 17). This, however, would not have been true if these branches had not expanded their volume of business (loans plus deposit balances) beyond Rs 1 million. Average transaction costs of a typical branch were 3.3 percent and average financial costs were 4.7 percent. However, such a branch would have suffered diseconomies of scale on transaction costs until its

Table 16—Deposit growth rates of nationalized commercial banks in India during 1980-85, according to branch groups

Branch Group/City	1980-85 Increase in Total Branch Deposits			
	Prior to 1970	Over 1970-75	Over 1975-80	Over All Three Periods
	(percent)			
Branch group				
Rural	114.8	154.3	268.6	162.7
Semiurban	94.2	138.0	220.7	116.1
Urban	87.4	139.6	210.2	111.6
Metropolitan	83.7	139.4	201.7	105.0
City				
Bombay	90.8	144.8	232.2	107.4
Delhi	92.6	147.7	204.4	116.7
Calcutta	58.4	130.0	177.5	84.2
Madras	76.9	149.2	196.8	99.1

Source: Gothoskar 1989.
Notes: Rural branches are those with centers of population under 10,000; semiurban branches have population centers of 10,000-50,000.

volume of business reached about Rs 1 million (Figure 5), after which it would rapidly reap economies of scale that would continue even beyond a volume of business of Rs 60 million.

Rural Institutional Finance System, India

In the two decades since 1961/62, the rural institutional finance system has performed well as far as financial deepening of the rural sector is concerned (Desai and Namboodiri 1991). But its performance is modest

Table 17—Estimated parameters of the log-log inverse transaction cost function for rural branches of the nationalized commercial banks, India

Dependent Variable	Con-stant	Coefficients Related to		$\bar{R}^2$	Scale Param-eter	Number of Obser-vations
		Loans Outstanding and Deposit Balances	Inverse of Loans Outstanding and Deposit Balances			
Transaction costs	0.023	0.664[a] (5.253)	-462.243 (-0.299)	0.968	0.68[b]	9

Notes: Figures in parentheses are t-values.
[a]Significant at 1 percent.
[b]Significantly less than 1, implying scale economies.

Figure 5—Behavior of scale economies in transaction costs of sample branches of the nationalized commercial banks in India, mid-1980s

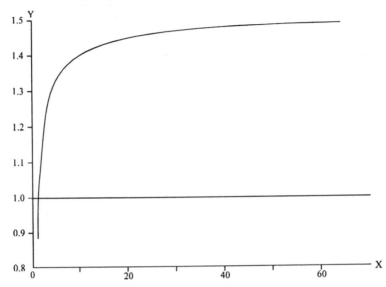

Source: Derived from Table 17.
Notes: Y = Reciprocal of elasticity of transaction costs with respect to volume of business.
X = Volume of business (loans plus deposit balances in Rs million).

regarding the proportion of agricultural output and national domestic product (NDP) financed. The number of functions it performs is also modest. Despite this, the system has been viable and has not suffered from scale diseconomies in transaction costs. It has increased the use of fertilizer, irrigation, other agricultural investment, and productivity. Not only has the density of rural financial institutions and farm-level credit increased, but also loans for distribution of agricultural inputs, cooperative marketing, and processing of agricultural produce. For India as a whole, however, loan delinquency is high, and scale economies in transaction costs have not been fully achieved. Had these disparate performances in density, coverage of farmers, scale and scope of farm loans, and multiproduct operations not occurred, these institutions would have had a much larger impact on agricultural investments and productivity and on profitability and loans recovery.

Macro Indicators. The rural institutional finance system consists of vertically organized cooperatives, cooperative land development banks, nationalized commercial banks, and regional rural banks. For India as a whole, rural loans and deposits as a percentage of agricultural output and value added have continuously increased since 1961/62, more sharply for rural deposits than for rural loans. Over the 1961/62-1985/86 period, the proportion of rural deposits as a share of agricultural output (28 percent) and of NDP (32 percent) is much higher than the proportion of rural loans to agricultural output and NDP (12 and 14 percent, respectively). Loans to the agricultural production subsystem—farm-level loans (direct agricultural credit)—as a percentage of agricultural output was 11 percent and 12 percent of NDP. These percentages are much lower than those in other developing countries like Brazil, Malaysia, Pakistan, and Thailand.

Density. In each five-year period during 1961/62-1985/86, the ratio of institution offices per 1,000 hectares declined from 1.51 to 1.25, to 1.23, to 1.1, and then to 1.0 because primary agricultural cooperative credit societies (PACS) were reorganized to cover a larger number of villages. Each PACS office became larger but there were fewer of them. This was done so that each PACS would have sufficient loan business to enable it to hire a full-time paid secretary. But, as will be shown later, this has not improved the PACS viability or facilitated scale economies in transaction costs. This suggests that increasing the size of PACS to incorporate a larger number of villages (and hence a larger area of operations and volume of loan business) does not necessarily improve their functioning. To the contrary, encouraging smaller PACS with more intensified, multiproduct operations would be a better strategy, as is borne out in the discussion of a previous study.[18] Moreover, while the density of branches of cooperative land development banks and rural and semiurban branches of commercial banks increased, their rate of growth varied significantly from one five-year period to another, suggesting a two-pronged future strategy of more sustained growth in density and more intensive and diversified operations. This strategy would reinforce the impact of banking infrastructure on agricultural and rural development because the supply of rural deposits and the demand for rural loans respond more favorably to accessibility to banking infrastructure than to higher interest rates.

Size of Rural Deposits and Loans. The annual average of rural deposits in constant prices was Rs 47.4 billion for the period 1961/62-1985/86. The annual compound growth rate was 18 percent. Moreover, the annual average of rural deposits increased over the five-year periods, but the annual compound growth rate in these deposits increased dramatically, then declined drastically, then improved substantially, and finally declined significantly (Table 18).

The annual average of rural loans in constant prices during 1961/62-1985/86 was Rs 30.5 billion. The compound growth rate in these loans was about 11 percent per year, but the annual compound growth fluctuated greatly from one period to another.

The rural credit-deposit ratio was more than 100 percent in the first period, based on Table 18. However, this ratio continuously declined from 94 percent in 1966/67-1970/71 to 69 percent in 1971/72-75/76, and then to 56 percent in the second half of the 1970s and the first half

---

[18]B. M. Desai 1983a shows that multifunctional PACS experienced scale economies in transaction costs, but this was not the case with unifunctional PACS in which farm-level loans are the PACS only function.

Table 18—Size and growth of rural deposits and rural loans in the rural institutional finance system, India, 1961/62-1985/86

Period	Rural Deposits		Rural Loans	
	Annual Average	Compound Growth Rate	Annual Average	Compound Growth Rate
	(1970/71 Rs billion)	(percent)	(1970/71 Rs billion)	(percent)
1961/62-1965/66	4.64	5.03	7.33	5.17
1966/67-1970/71	14.09	61.94	15.18	30.83
1971/72-1975/76	31.29	3.02	26.67	3.27
1976/77-1980/81	67.46	13.22	51.68	11.80
1981/82-1985/86	113.90	7.11	64.58	7.26
1961/62-1985/86	47.36	18.15	30.54	11.33

Source: Desai and Namboodiri 1991.
Notes: Annual averages are in constant Rs billion at 1970/71 prices.

of the 1980s. At the end of the 25 years, the credit-deposit ratio was 65 percent. Moreover, the ratio of incremental rural credit to rural deposits was 0.63 in the second period, 0.48 in the third period, 0.44 in the fourth period, and 0.26 in the fifth period. This suggests that the rural institutional finance system in India has been able to achieve a large net transfer of financial resources from the rural sector. This conclusion will hold even in the face of high loan overdues because under such circumstances no new loans will be made to delinquent borrowers. Inasmuch as the incremental rural credit-rural deposit ratio was considerably lower than 0.6 in the last two periods, it may also imply that the rural sector was deprived of adequate credit. Further, by the early 1980s only about one-tenth of agricultural NDP, one-fourth of the variable cost, and one-third of the capital formation in agriculture were financed by the RFIs.

Functional Structure of Agricultural Loans. There are two types of structures for agricultural loans. One is the pattern for all agricultural loans—those for the agricultural inputs distribution subsystem (AIS), the agricultural production subsystem (APS), and the agricultural marketing and processing subsystem (AMPS)—in which direct and indirect agricultural credit can be classified. The other is the pattern of APS loans—loans for current production growth and stability (CPGS), which mainly include loans for crop production, soil and moisture improvements, irrigation assets, farm implements and equipment, plow animals and carts; current production diversification and growth (CPDG), which mainly include loans for dairy farming, sheep farming, poultry, and other livestock; and current production loss minimization (CPLM), which includes rescheduling of past loans and debt redemption. While data on the first type of classification are available for all RFIs, data on the latter are available only for PACS and cooperative land development banks.

Although APS loans were dominant throughout the period, the annual average of AIS and AMPS loans increased continuously (Table 19). But the annual compound growth rate in APS loans was lower than that in either AMPS or AIS loans. These rather disparate performances suggest an imbalance between the demand for and supply of farm inputs encouraged through APS and AIS loans, respectively. It also suggests a lack of sustained credit support for an activity crucial to transfer of new technology to APS.

The pattern of APS loans shown in Table 20 reveals that CPGS loans advanced by cooperatives clearly dominated, followed distantly by CPLM loans, and then CPDG loans.[19] Over the four periods, the average amount of CPGS loans increased continuously, while that of CPLM loans varied significantly. The annual compound growth rate in CPGS loans increased quite dramatically in the second half of the 1960s, then it declined and finally marginally increased. Such large fluctuations in growth, in so far as they are caused by external factors, are unfortunate because they cause similar fluctuations in the adoption of new technology by farmers.

Association of Agricultural Progress with RFIs. Both agricultural productivity and agricultural investments (such as fertilizer use, minor irrigation development, plow animals, animal husbandry, tillage implements, irrigation equipment, threshers, and tractors) are positively associated with density of RFIs, rural deposits, AIS loans, APS loans, AMPS loans, CPGS loans of cooperatives, CPDG loans of cooperatives, and CPLM loans of cooperatives.[20]

Delinquency Rate of APS Loans. This is measured as 100 minus loans recovered as a percent of those due. The delinquency rate was about 45 percent during 1973/74-1981/82. This rate was the highest, 48 percent, in the severe drought year of 1979/80. In four out of nine years, the rate declined, but it never went below 43 percent. The delinquency rate could be lowered to about 35 percent if it were measured as 100 minus loans recovered as a percent of loans outstanding.[21] Such a measure would to some extent allow for loan recoveries after the maturity date, which usually coincides with the harvest time. Nonetheless, even this rate is likely to be high.

The reasons for the high rate of delinquency are complex and varied. The following are some of the important ones: (1) natural factors like drought and floods; (2) inadequate increases in production and marketable surplus; (3) mismatches between the time schedule fixed for loan recovery and the time when farmers can repay loans; (4) inadequate credit resulting from an age-old formula used to determine the scale of

---

[19]The relative importance of these three types of loans would be reversed if data on commercial banks were also considered, which was not possible because data on the three types of APS loans made by commercial banks were not available.

[20]For a similar finding based on more disaggregated data of major states in India, see Desai, Gupta, and Singh 1988.

[21]This was not computed because the required data for commercial banks were not available.

Table 19—Pattern of agricultural loans of the rural institutional finance system, India, 1961/62-1981/82

Period	AIS Loans Outstanding			APS Loans Outstanding			AMPS Loans Outstanding		
	Percent	Annual Average	Annual Compound Growth Rate	Percent	Annual Average	Annual Compound Growth Rate	Percent	Annual Average	Annual Compound Growth Rate
		(Rs billion)	(percent)		(Rs billion)	(percent)		(Rs billion)	(percent)
1961/62-1965/66	0.0	0.0	0.0	94.50	6.93	5.67	5.50	0.40	1.33
1966/67-1970/71	8.00	1.04	a	87.10	11.37	24.68	5.00	0.65	59.38
1971/72-1975/76	13.90	3.04	11.81	81.30	17.81	3.40	4.80	1.04	11.51
1976/77-1980/81	12.20	4.72	12.91	83.30	32.25	11.35	4.50	1.74	15.05
1961/62-1981/82	14.80	3.37	12.51	80.60	18.39	10.69	4.60	1.06	15.32

Source: Desai and Namboodiri 1991.

Notes: The period 1981/82-1985/86 is not covered because separate data for AIS, APS, and AMPS were unavailable. Annual averages are in constant Rs billion at 1970/71 prices.

    AIS = Agricultural Inputs Distribution Subsystem
    APS = Agricultural Production Subsystem
    AMPS = Agricultural Marketing and Processing Subsystem

aNot computed because these loans began in 1969.

Table 20—Pattern of loans advanced by the cooperatives for the agricultural production subsystem (APS), India, 1961/62-1981/82

Period	CPGS Loans Outstanding			CPDG Loans Outstanding			CPLM Loans Outstanding		
	Percent	Annual Average	Annual Compound Growth Rate	Percent	Annual Average	Annual Compound Growth Rate	Percent	Annual Average	Annual Compound Growth Rate
		(Rs billion)	(percent)		(Rs billion)	(percent)		(Rs billion)	(percent)
1961/62-1965/66	98.70	4.72	1.16	0.00	0.00	0.00	1.30	0.06	-12.09
1966/67-1970/71	99.70	5.67	14.23	0.00	0.00	0.00	0.30	0.02	-23.96
1971/72-1975/76	98.90	6.55	1.93	0.00	0.00	0.00	1.10	0.07	129.33
1976/77-1980/81	93.60	8.97	2.78	2.20	0.21	0.02	4.20	0.40	3.44
1961/62-1981/82	96.80	6.69	4.44	0.90	0.07	0.02	2.30	0.15	13.50

Source: Desai and Namboodiri 1991.
Notes: CPGS = Current production growth and stability
CPDG = Current production diversification and growth
CPLM = Current production loss minimization

finance; (5) unavailability of complementary credit such as crop loans, which enable term loans to be efficiently utilized, (6) unavailable, inadequate, or untimely availability of inputs and extension services; (7) inadequate supervision and attention to selection; and (8) perhaps, low interest rates.

Some of these factors can be dealt with by improving rates of return on farmers' investments and their repayment capacity, and some by perfecting the loan appraisal and monitoring processes of RFIs. The former would include government investment in or institutional credit for developing irrigated and watershed-based farming in rainfed areas and marketing of complementary inputs by supporting them through AIS credit. Rather than writing off past loans, adoption of these policy measures should be a priority. That some of these do lower delinquency rates is revealed by the finding that delinquency decreases with an increase in rural deposits, AIS loans, APS loans (especially for current production growth and stability and for current production diversification and growth), and AMPS loans.

Net Margins and Unit Transaction Costs. During the study period, all the RFIs had positive net margins (Table 21). State cooperative banks (SCBs) were most profitable, followed by the district central cooperative banks (DCCBs), Indian scheduled commercial banks (ISCBs), cooperative land development banks (CLDBs), primary agricultural cooperative credit societies (PACS), and regional rural banks (RRBs). In the first three of the four periods of five years each, the positive net margin declined or remained constant for all RFIs, except CLDBs, where it first improved and then declined. In the remaining period (1976/77-1980/81), the average net margin improved for SCBs, CLDBs, and ISCBs, but declined for DCCBs and PACS, becoming negative for PACS in one period.

Average transaction costs increased for SCBs and PACS over the four periods (Table 21). For DCCBs and ISCBs, it increased up to the third period, then declined in the fourth period. For CLDBs, it declined in the second period and then increased. Overall, unit transaction costs were highest for SCBs (3.48 percent), followed by ISCBs (1.46 percent), then PACS (1.26 percent), DCCBs (1.06 percent), RRBs (0.97 percent), and finally CLDBs (0.54 percent). These findings suggest that there is no one-to-one correspondence between unit profit and unit transaction costs.

Scale Economies in Transaction Costs. In all RFIs, except PACS, constant return to scale in their transaction costs prevailed during the period as a whole (Table 22). In other words, their transaction costs increased in the same proportion as their scale of operations increased. PACS, however, suffered from scale diseconomies during the entire period. DCCBs and ISCBs also experienced scale diseconomies, but only during the first subperiod. In the 1970s, DCCBs had the scope to achieve scale economies, while ISCBs already enjoyed scale economies.

Agricultural Bank of Sudan (ABS), Sudan

The Agricultural Bank of Sudan (ABS) is one of the five institutional financing agencies serving the agricultural sector in Sudan (A. H. Ahmed 1980; Ahmed and Adams 1987). ABS not only supplies credit and

Table 21—Unit profit and unit transaction costs of RFIs, India, 1961/62-1981/82

Type of Institution	1961/62-1965/66	1966/67-1970/71	1971/72-1975/76	1976/77-1980/81	1961/62-1981/82
			(percent)		
Unit profit[a]					
State cooperative banks (SCBs)	3.67	3.45	3.28	3.60	3.51
District central cooperative banks (DCCBs)	0.52	0.46	0.46	0.41	0.43
Primary agricultural cooperative credit societies (PACS)	0.66	0.61	0.35	-0.11	0.25
Cooperative land development banks (CLDBs)	0.28	0.30	0.25	0.33	0.30
Indian scheduled commercial banks (ISCBs)[b]	0.48	0.35	0.35	0.40	0.40
Regional rural banks (RRBs)[c]	...	...	...	0.11	0.11
Unit transaction costs[a]					
State cooperative banks (SCBs)	1.92	2.49	4.03	4.23	3.48
District central cooperative banks (DCCBs)	0.59	0.88	1.23	1.20	1.06
Primary agricultural cooperative credit societies (PACS)	1.02	1.17	1.20	1.38	1.26
Cooperative land development banks (CLDBs)	0.33	0.28	0.53	0.63	0.54
Indian scheduled commercial banks (ISCBs)[b]	1.12	1.44	1.70	1.41	1.46
Regional rural banks (RRBs)[c]	...	...	...	1.03	0.97

Source: Desai and Namboodiri 1991.
[a]Computed as a percentage of all assets plus liabilities, excluding contra items.
[b]Computed for all types of branches serving all sectors, because separate data for rural and semiurban branches are not available.
[c]Data are only available for 1976/77-1981/82, although these banks came into existence in 1975.

collects some deposits, but it also supplies modern farm inputs, including extension services and some marketing services. This functional structure may have enabled two of its branches selected for study to become viable—both in explicit and implicit terms—the first in the sense of earning a positive average net margin and the second as revealed by high loan collection rates.[22] Moreover, both these branches enjoyed scale economies in their transaction costs, although the results suggest that there is considerable scope for enlarging the scale of operations. This has not been achieved due to the irregularity of financial support from the government and international agencies. The basis of these conclusions is explained below.

ABS was established in 1959 by the government. In 1979, its authorized capital was LS 15 million, while its paid-up capital was only LS 9 million.

[22]These findings are at variance with the authors' findings largely because the latter do not consider the measure of unit net margin, besides other reasons discussed previously.

Table 22—Scale parameters and implied economies or diseconomies in transaction costs of RFIs, India, 1961/62-1981/82

Institution	1961/62-1970/71	1971/72-1981/82	1961/62-1981/82
State cooperative banks (SCBs)	1.05 (CRS)	0.94 (CRS)	1.81 (CRS)
District central cooperative banks (DCCBs)	2.21 (SDE)	0.99 (CRS)	1.58 (CRS)
Primary agricultural cooperative credit societies (PACS)	1.28 (SDE)	1.42 (SDE)	1.34 (SDE)
Cooperative land development banks (CLDBs)	0.81 (CRS)	1.98 (CRS)	1.30 (CRS)
Indian scheduled commercial banks (ISCBs)	1.68 (SDE)	0.83 (SE)	1.12 (CRS)
Regional rural banks (RRBs)	. . .	. . .	0.91 (CRS)[a]

Source: Desai and Namboodiri 1991.

Notes: Scale parameters are derived from econometric cost functions in which transaction costs is a dependent variable and assets plus liabilities, excluding contra items, is an independent variable. Both are measured in constant 1970/71 prices. The agricultural NDP deflator is used to obtain these values in real terms.

CRS = constant returns to scale, implying neither scale economies nor diseconomies, because scale parameter is statistically not significantly different from 1.

SDE = scale diseconomies, implying decreasing returns to scale, because scale parameter is statistically and significantly greater than 1.

SE = scale economies, implying increasing returns to scale, because scale parameter is statistically and significantly less than 1.

[a]For 1977/78-1981/82 only.

The government of Sudan paid 40 percent and the Bank of Sudan paid the rest. ABS's main sources of funds, in order of importance, were loan recoveries, own capital, some deposits, and "irregular insertions of external funds from the government and from donors" (Ahmed and Adams 1987, 3).

ABS supplies credit, improved seeds, fertilizers, insecticides, extension services, and physical services such as handling, storage, and marketing, besides market information to its borrowers. It extends these services to "support agriculture and other activities that are incidental, accessory, ancillary, and subsidiary thereto by offering assistance in cash, kind, goods, or services to approved persons who are primarily engaged in agriculture or allied and subsidiary industries" (A. H. Ahmed 1980, 76-77). For all of its services, ABS gives preference to small- and medium-sized farmers and to agricultural cooperatives.

ABS has two departments: agricultural credit and financial. Through its network of 24 branches, ABS extends credit and other services to individual farmers under government and semigovernment agricultural schemes and through agricultural cooperatives. Credit is largely extended to those farmers who can provide satisfactory collateral. ABS's resources are mainly channeled to the importation of farm machinery and other farm inputs and to short- and medium-term loans in the mechanized rainfed and irrigated areas.

A. H. Ahmed (1980) selected two branches to study lending costs, among other aspects. Wad Medani is irrigated and Dilling is a rainfed area. For Dilling, Ahmed provides data on revenues from various activities and financial costs, while for Wad Medani he provides data on lending rates and financial costs.

Based on the data available for Dilling, the measures relevant for determining the net margins of this branch are presented in Table 23. Even this rainfed branch had positive average net margins during 1975-77. Unit margins and transaction costs varied from year to year, but unit financial costs did not, mainly because of irregularity in the availability of funds, especially for new loans and imports of inputs. Nevertheless, the branch was able to reduce its unit transaction costs by more than 50 percent in 1977. At 0.38, the scale parameter during 1974-77 was considerably less than 1 (Table 24). In other words, such a parameter suggests a scope to reduce costs by expanding the scale of operations, which has largely been constrained by the unavailability of funds. In order to overcome this, the branch, with the assistance of ABS, should not only mobilize deposits, but should also strongly solicit more sustained financial support from the government and the Bank of Sudan. This is especially so because the loan collection rate of this branch is very high—78-90 percent during the period 1965-77.

These analytical conclusions also hold for Wad Medani, the irrigated branch, though the numerical values of unit net margin and unit transaction costs vary considerably. Moreover, the unit net margin for the Wad Medani branch is lower because it only accounts for interest revenue, as data on other revenues are not reported in A. H. Ahmed

Table 23—Various costs, gross margin, and net margin of the Dilling Branch of the Agricultural Bank of Sudan, Sudan, 1975-77

Variable in Real Terms[a]	Three-Year Average	1975	1976	1977
	(percent)			
Unit transaction costs[b]	13.11	18.51	19.87	9.19
Unit total revenue[b]	33.10	29.92	51.02	27.23
Unit financial costs[b]	3.00	3.00	3.00	3.00
Unit gross margin[b]	30.10	26.92	48.02	24.33
Unit net margin[b]	17.01	8.41	28.15	15.14

Source: A. H. Ahmed 1980.

[a]Real terms are derived by applying the consumer price deflator to a base year of 1980/81. The agricultural GDP deflator could not be used because data were unavailable.

[b]Variables are computed as a percent of loans advanced plus the value of farm input operations. The value was estimated by applying the share of this branch's advances in total advances to the total value of farm input operations of the Agricultural Bank of Sudan.

Table 24—Estimated parameters of the double-log transaction cost function for the Dilling branch of the Agricultural Bank of Sudan, Sudan

Dependent Variable in Real Terms	Unit Costs[a]	Marginal Costs[a]	Constant	Loans Made Plus Input Operations in Real Terms	$\bar{R}^2$	Scale Parameter	Number of Observations
	(percent)						
Transaction costs	14.75	5.60	5.914	0.379[b] (2.889)	0.710	0.38[c]	4

Note: Figures in parentheses are t-values.
[a]These costs for each of the four years are as follows:

Year	Unit Costs	Marginal Costs
	(percent)	
1974	25.40	9.65
1975	18.51	7.03
1976	19.87	7.55
1977	9.19	3.49

[b]Significant at 20 percent.
[c]Statistically and significantly less than 1, which suggests the existence of scale economies.

1980. For this branch, however, the net margin increased continuously, which is exclusively due to the continuous decline in its unit transaction costs (Table 25). Lastly, the magnitude of the scale parameter in Table 26 suggests that this branch also has the scope to expand its scale of operations to utilize more fully its administrative resources.

Bank for Agriculture and Agricultural Cooperatives (BAAC), Thailand

BAAC has extended loans not only for agricultural production, but also for encouraging the supply of farm inputs as well as procurement and purchase of farm produce (Meyer, Baker, and Onchon 1979). This has been possible because of its strategy to extend loans to individual farmers as well as to cooperatives. Perhaps as a result it has achieved a lower loan delinquency rate, lower unit transaction costs, and scale economies in these costs. For these achievements, it has depended not only on refinancing but also on deposits from commercial banks and its own clients.

BAAC is one of the four rural financial institutions in Thailand, but in terms of volume it is the single most important source of formal credit for Thai agriculture. It was established in 1966 to take over the cooperative lending activities of the former Bank of Cooperatives and to institute direct credit to farmers. BAAC's capital is largely from the government (about 77 percent), followed by accumulated profit (18 percent),

Table 25—Various costs, gross margin, and net margin of the Wad Medani branch of the Agricultural Bank of Sudan, Sudan, 1975-77

Variable in Real Tems[a]	Three-Year Average	1975	1976	1977
	(percent)			
Unit transaction costs[b]	2.98	5.51	3.39	2.09
Unit total revenue[b]	8.83	8.79	8.76	8.88
Unit financial costs[b]	3.00	3.00	3.00	3.00
Unit gross margin[b]	5.83	5.79	5.76	5.88
Unit net margin[b]	2.85	0.28	2.37	3.79

Source: A. H. Ahmed 1980.

[a]Real terms are derived by applying the consumer price deflator to a base year of 1980/81. The agricultural GDP deflator could not be used because data were unavailable.

[b]Variables are computed as a percentage of loans advanced plus the value of farm input operations. The value was estimated by applying the share of this branch's advances in total advances to the total value of farm input operations of the Agricultural Bank of Sudan. Data on transaction costs for 1975 and 1976 were obtained by extrapolating observed values of 1974 and 1977.

Table 26—Estimated parameters of the double-log transaction cost function for the Wad Medani branch of the Agricultural Bank of Sudan, Sudan

Dependent Variable in Real Terms	Unit Costs[a]	Marginal Costs[a]	Constant	Coefficient Related to Loans Made Plus Input Operations in Real Terms	$\bar{R}^2$	Scale Parameter	Number of Observations
	(percent)						
Transaction costs	3.64	0.36	9.205	0.102[b] (2.889)	0.607	0.10[c]	4

Note: Figures in parentheses are t-values. Real terms are derived by applying the GDP deflator to a base year of 1972/73.

[a]These costs for each of the four years are as follows:

Year	Unit Costs	Marginal Costs
	(percent)	
1974	8.95	0.89
1975	5.51	0.55
1976	3.39	0.34
1977	2.09	0.21

[b]Significant at 20 percent.

[c]Statistically and significantly less than 1, which suggests the existence of scale economies.

reserves (4 percent), and then the cooperatives' and individuals' share capital contributions (1 percent). Its sources of loanable funds include commercial bank deposits (51 percent), followed by rediscounted promissory notes with the Central Bank (the Bank of Thailand) (16 percent), deposits from the investing public (15 percent), farmers' loan compensatory deposits (7 percent), borrowing from abroad (6 percent), and other funds (5 percent).

BAAC has a network of 58 provincial branches and 331 field offices covering most of the country's 72 provinces. Its lending to individual farmers includes short-, medium-, and long-term loans. It also lends to cooperatives and farmers' associations for lending to members and "for financing cooperative inventories, rice purchases from members, and construction of physical facilities" (Meyer, Baker, and Onchon 1979, 18). In fact, in early years, a substantial part of its loans went to these cooperatives and farmers' associations. This suggests that BAAC extended its financial services not only to encourage demand for farm inputs and supply of increased farm produce but also to encourage farm input supply and farm produce procurement demand. This, in itself, may have led to a high loan collection rate of more than 70 percent in five out of the eight years for which data are available in the 1970s.[23] Perhaps another reason for such a high rate is intensive administrative supervision and its associated high transaction costs, which enabled this bank to control loan delinquency. Indeed, as administrative costs increased, the loan delinquency rate decreased; the coefficient of correlation between these variables is –0.6215.

BAAC earned a positive unit net margin in 1976 (Table 27). This margin is underestimated because it does not account for noninterest revenues that the bank may have earned.

Table 27—Various costs and viability of the Bank for Agriculture and Agricultural Cooperatives, Thailand, 1976

Variable in Real Terms	1975
	(percent)
Unit transaction costs[a]	2.38
Unit total revenue[b]	3.26
Unit financial costs[b]	5.89
Unit gross margin[b]	2.63
Unit net margin[b]	0.25

Source: Meyer, Baker, and Onchon 1979.
Note: Real terms are derived by applying the GDP deflator to a base year of 1972/73.
[a]Unit transaction costs are computed as a percentage of loans outstanding plus deposit balances.
[b]Both unit financial costs and interest revenue are estimated from the data given in the study from which this short case study is prepared. Both these variables are divided by 2 to make them comparable with unit transaction costs.

---

[23]Even in the remaining three years of the 1970s, this rate was over 51 percent.

BAAC also enjoyed scale economies in its transaction costs (Table 28). Moreover, its unit transaction costs continuously declined. Both suggest that BAAC has been successful in controlling administrative costs, but they also suggest that BAAC could improve its viability further by expanding its scale of operations under the given interest rate structure.

All Agricultural Cooperatives, Thailand

Agricultural cooperatives have a long history in Thailand, as in the rest of Asia (Thailand, Ministry of Agriculture and Cooperatives 1979). They are organized along the lines of the Raiffaisen model and were initiated and promoted by the government. A number of cooperatives now exist, which are vertically organized and financially supported by the government, as well as BAAC, but they do not have a central financing agency of their own.

The primary agricultural cooperatives (consisting of general purpose societies, societies in cooperation with other agencies, animal-raising cooperatives, and other special types of cooperatives) had positive net margins during 1973-78. In addition, they provided useful services such as credit, deposits, marketing, farm input supplies, and extension. Moreover, these cooperatives achieved scale economies in their aggregate administrative and financial costs.

The history of the cooperative movement in Thailand dates back to 1916 when the first cooperative was formed in a rural area as a village credit cooperative along the lines of the Raiffaisen model. It was initiated by the government, which was still an absolute monarchy. After the first Cooperative Societies Act in 1928, other types of cooperatives were also formed. Among these are land hire-purchase, land settlement, land improvement, marketing and processing, consumers', thrift and credit, and fishery and animal-raising cooperatives, though credit cooperatives still predominate.

Cooperatives of all types are promoted to increase income and improve the standard of living of their members. The government takes the role of supplying technical training and servicing, including financial support where needed, which is necessary for the effective development of the cooperative movement.

At the initial stages, the government directly provided the cooperatives with funds to be loaned to their members against land mortgages and guarantors. In 1943, the Bank for Cooperatives was organized to serve as a financing center of the agricultural cooperatives and to take the place of direct lendings by the government. It was superseded in 1966 by the Bank for Agriculture and Agricultural Cooperatives in order to widen the scope of operations to include loans to individual farmers, as well as agricultural cooperatives.

The cooperatives are vertically organized at three levels: primary societies at the local level, secondary societies at the provincial level, and apex societies at the national level.[24] A primary society consists of

---

[24]At the provincial level, there are secondary federations of primary-level cooperatives. Both primary and secondary societies are federated at the national level by the formation of a marketing cooperative. Hence, no central financing agency exists at the provincial or national level for cooperatives.

Table 28—Estimated parameters of the log-log inverse transaction cost function for the Bank for Agriculture and Agricultural Cooperatives, Thailand

Dependent Variable in Real Terms	Unit Costs[a]	Marginal Costs[a]	Constant	Coefficient Related to		$\bar{R}^2$	Scale Parameter	Number of Observations
				Loans Outstanding Plus Deposit Balances in Real Terms	Inverse of Loans Outstanding and Deposit Balances in Real Terms			
	(percent)							
Transaction costs	3.10	1.95	-2.706	687.722[b] (5.915)	0.872[c] (2.466)	0.953	0.63[d]	7

Notes: Figures in parentheses are t-values. Real terms are derived by applying the agricultural GDP deflator with a base year of 1972/73.

[a] These costs for each of the four years are as follows:

Year	Unit Transaction Costs	Marginal Transaction Costs
	(percent)	
1970	6.30	3.97
1971	3.81	2.40
1972	3.35	2.11
1973	3.22	2.03
1974	3.15	1.98
1975	2.90	1.83
1976	2.38	1.50

[b] Significant at 1 percent.
[c] Significant at 10 percent.
[d] Statistically and significantly less than 1, which implies the prevalence of scale economies.

individual farmers at the district or local level. The functions of such a society are to extend credit, marketing, farm input supplies, farm extension services, processing, water management, occupation promotion, and funeral services to its members.

During 1973-79, the number of primary cooperatives varied from 555 to 823 and their membership from 324,043 to 685,494. By 1979, although these societies served only 15 percent of the total farm population, they were considered the best-organized farm institution. In 1974 and 1975, the number of cooperatives declined because of amalgamations. The main sources of loanable resources of these cooperatives are share capital, reserve funds, borrowings, and deposits.

These cooperatives were viable from 1973 to 1978 (Table 29). Their average total costs (transaction plus financial) increased until 1975 and thereafter declined steadily through 1978. Their unit revenue from all activities showed similar behavior. Consequently, their unit net margin first improved and then deteriorated, although it did not turn negative in any of the six years under study. In three out of the six years, these societies enjoyed scale economies in their aggregate costs and in some years they had neither scale economies nor diseconomies. In other words, the increase in their costs was proportionate to the increase in their value of operations. Taking all six of the years together, these societies realized constant returns to scale (Table 30), but both their viability and realization of scale economies could be improved if their financial constraints could be alleviated, management improved, and extension services expanded by forming their own central financing agency at the provincial level.

Agricultural Credit Cooperatives, Thailand

Agricultural credit cooperatives of Thailand are essentially primary-level credit cooperatives, although they do undertake some noncredit operations such as farm input supplies and extension (Thailand, Ministry of

Table 29—Aggregate costs, aggregate revenue, and net margin of all agricultural cooperatives, Thailand, 1973-78

Variable in Real Terms	Mean	1973	1974	1975	1976	1977	1978
				(percent)			
Unit aggregate costs (administrative plus financial costs)[a]	14.45	9.68	16.57	18.30	15.98	14.34	12.50
Unit aggregate revenue[a]	15.43	11.29	18.64	19.11	17.04	15.25	13.10
Unit net margin[a]	0.98	1.61	2.07	0.81	1.06	0.91	0.60
Marginal aggregate costs[b]	9.83	37.27	33.47	18.30	7.19	4.73	10.50

Source: Thailand, Ministry of Agriculture and Cooperatives, Cooperatives Promotion Department 1979.

Note: Real terms are derived by applying the agricultural GDP deflator with a base year of 1972/73.

[a]These variables are computed as a percentage of loanable resources plus assets.

Table 30—Estimated parameters of the cubic aggregate cost function for all agricultural cooperatives, Thailand

Dependent Variable in Real Terms	Constant	Coefficients Related to				$\bar{R}^2$	Scale Parameter	Number of Observations
		Operating Capital Plus Assets in Real Terms	Square of Operating Capital Plus Assets in Real Terms	Cubic of Operating Capital Plus Assets in Real Terms				
Transaction plus interest costs	−590.385	0.736[a] (0.321)	−0.00016[b] (−2.079)	0.000000012[c] (1.685)		0.979	0.68[d]	6

Notes: Figures in parentheses are t-values. Real terms are derived by applying the agricultural GDP deflator with a base year of 1972/73.
[a]Significant at 10 percent.
[b]Significant at 20 percent.
[c]Significant at 40 percent.
[d]Statistically but not significantly different from 1, suggesting that scale economies have not been fully reaped.

Agriculture and Cooperatives 1979). They have been constrained from undertaking operations such as short-term lending, farm input supplies, and farm produce purchase on a large scale due to lack of finances and managerial guidance. Despite this, these cooperatives are viable and are reaping scale economies in their aggregate costs; both could be improved if these constraints were relaxed and if the loan collection rate (which at present is modest) could be improved, as well as the rate of return on farm investments associated with new technological inputs.

These cooperatives differ from those discussed in the previous section. They are truly agricultural credit cooperatives, while the previous case included general-purpose cooperatives, societies in cooperation with other agencies, animal-raising cooperatives, and societies of special forms. A common feature of all of the cooperatives covered in the two case studies is that they are organized at the primary level.

This case study is exclusively based on cross-section data of 41 societies surveyed in 1972. The purpose of these cooperatives is to form an institution to extend an integrated package to assist farmers to improve their standard of living. This is being achieved through the provision of credit, marketing, farm input supplies, extension, processing, and other services to the members. However, in reality, agricultural credit has claimed the major portion of their activities in achieving their goal. For example, in 1972, the main source of revenue of an agricultural cooperative was interest earnings on loans (94.69 percent). This is similar throughout the nine provinces from which the sample was drawn.[25] Thus, for all practical purposes, these cooperatives were credit societies. They extended both short- and long-term loans to farmer-members, the former being only 18 percent of the total. The main sources of their working capital or loanable resources were share capital, reserve funds, borrowings, deposits, and others. The loan collection rate was only about 49 percent in 1972. This rate ranged from 44 to 54 percent across the nine different administrative areas.

Utilizing the reported grouped data of the agricultural cooperatives from the nine different areas, Table 31 reports average total costs, unit revenue, and average net margin of these cooperatives. The positive average net margin is an important achievement, considering that these cooperatives are largely credit cooperatives.

The cooperatives in the sample could improve their profitability by enlarging their scale of operations and diversifying their loan portfolios without endangering the quality of these operations. They could also enlarge the scale of operations of their nonlending business activities, such as farm input supplies and farm produce purchase operations, which would be possible because these cooperatives have a scale parameter of 0.42 (Table 32). Moreover, such changes in their business operations would also improve loan collection rates through the higher rates of return on farm investment that would result from the use of modern

---

[25]In 1972, the share of these cooperatives in total institutional credit was about 32 percent, and their share in the number of farmers financed by all RFIs was 23 percent.

Table 31—Aggregate costs, revenue, and net margin of a sample of agricultural credit cooperatives, Thailand, 1972

Administrative Area	Unit Aggregate Costs[a]	Unit Revenue	Unit Net Margin[a]
	(percent)		
Ayudhaya	4.33	6.98	2.65
Chacheongsao	6.06	9.29	3.23
Udornthani	6.69	9.57	2.88
Nakorn-Rajsrima	5.60	7.93	2.33
Lampang	7.56	10.94	3.38
Pitsanuloke	6.25	8.78	2.53
Nakorn-Sawan	5.88	8.53	2.65
Petchabusi	6.12	8.34	2.22
Nakon-Srithammaraj	8.26	11.07	2.81
Average	6.11	8.81	2.70

Source: Thailand, Ministry of Agriculture and Cooperatives.
[a]Computed as a percentage of loanable resources divided by 2.

farm inputs and technology and from assured marketing facilities. Such improvements would be possible if the constraints of inadequate financing, lack of relevant managerial and extension services, and lack of coordination with other agencies were relaxed, as was discussed for the previous case study.

The National Agricultural Cooperative Federation (NACF), Republic of Korea

NACF is an apex institution in the Republic of Korea's system of cooperatives (Brake 1971; Korea, Republic of, NACF various years). NACF's main sources of funds are borrowing, deposits, and to some extent equity. It,

Table 32—Estimated parameters of the double-log aggregate cost function for agricultural credit cooperatives, Thailand, 1972

Dependent Variable per Society	Constant	Loanable Resources Plus Assets per Society	$\bar{R}^2$	Scale Parameter	Number of Observations
Aggregate costs (administrative plus financial)	5.757	0.423[a] (2.315)	0.352	0.42[b]	9

Note: Figures in parentheses are t-values.
[a]Significant at 10 percent.
[b]Statistically and significantly lower than 1, which implies prevalence of scale economies.

like the county and primary cooperatives, is multipurpose: it extends loans and provides input supply, produce marketing, and extension services. Nevertheless, NACF had negative net margins in both 1967 and 1970, although it broke even in 1975 and 1976. The reasons are largely related to (1) nonfinancial activities undertaken directly, rather than indirectly, by extending financial services to the lower-level cooperatives for input supplies and produce marketing; (2) inadequate decentralization; (3) inability to mobilize deposits despite upward revision in interest rates on deposit; and (4) a large amount of nonearning and costly assets like accounts receivable, advance payment, and inventory in its total assets. These suggest that net margins of an RFI are dependent on complex and interdependent factors. In addition to holding less costly and higher income-earning assets, reforms in nonprice policies and perhaps in interest rates on deposits would improve NACF's viability.

Cooperatives in the Republic of Korea have a long history. They were initiated under the Japanese occupation. During that time and after, reorganizations were made to benefit the farmers and agricultural development. The cooperatives are vertically organized. The Financial Associations were established in 1907 to extend credit services to farmers, whereas the Farmers' Associations were organized in 1920 to conduct purchasing and sales of commodities. Both these institutions were "run under the auspices and control of the government" (Korea, Republic of, NACF various years, 6). "Under Japanese control, a national cooperative federation was established to jointly handle banking and business activities for agriculture" (Brake 1971, 1).

But in 1956 the Financial Associations were reorganized into the Korean Agricultural Bank (KAB), dealing exclusively with institutional agricultural credit, and in 1957 the Agricultural Cooperatives (AC) were established through the reorganization of the Farmers' Associations. But, these two agricultural institutions "lacked close linkage and efficiency in operation due to duplication and competition in business activities. Therefore, harmony and cooperation between these institutions were imperative for the benefit of farmers as well as agricultural development" (Korea, Republic of, NACF various years, 6). In 1961, KAB and AC were merged into the present multipurpose cooperatives in compliance with the new Agricultural Cooperative Law.

These cooperatives are now vertically organized at three levels: the primary cooperatives at the township level, county cooperatives at county and city levels, and the federal organization (NACF) at the national level.

NACF's loanable resources constitute funds from (1) the government, including foreign loans and transfers; (2) deposits in its own banking system and borrowings from other banks, primarily the Bank of Korea; and (3) accumulation of its share capital and reserves. The credit-deposit ratio of NACF was much greater than 1.00—1.78 in 1967, 3.15 in 1970, 1.31 in 1975, and 1.33 in 1976.

NACF's banking and credit operations include both agricultural and nonagricultural deposits and loans for both individuals and institutions, mutual savings, credit supervision and farm management guidance, and linkages between credit and the farm supply and product marketing activities of this institution. The farm supply activities provide fertilizer, farm chemicals, seed, feed, farm machinery, tools and equipment, breeding livestock, and other production inputs. The product marketing activities include general marketing of members' agricultural products as well as operation of the marketing of government products purchased and sold for price stabilization purposes. It also handles sales and promotion of farm handiwork products such as straw mats, bamboo products, and other items. And finally, it also runs a mutual insurance program for life and fire insurance protection for policy-holding members.[26]

Despite the multipurpose nature of NACF, it had negative net margins in 1967 and 1970, the years for which relevant data are available (Table 33).[27] Because this finding appears contradictory to the proposed hypothesis, it needs to be analyzed further in spite of the limited data available. The following reasons for these losses seem possible.

- Perhaps NACF, as an open institution, undertook too many activities, rather than acting as a financial institution.
- In doing so, it may have decentralized too little, not only in appraising and monitoring loans, but also in undertaking non-credit operations that could have been promoted by extending financial services to its constituents at lower levels, namely, county cooperatives and primary cooperatives.
- The preceding two seem to have led to higher average transaction costs.
- Even unit financial costs seem high, and they were increasing. This resulted from higher interest rates on deposits (which were introduced under the interest-rate reforms of the mid-1960s) without increasing collection of deposits (Table 34).[28]
- The increase in average transaction costs was much smaller than increases in average financial costs and average revenue (Table 33). Moreover, unit financial costs increased more (21 percent) than unit revenue (16 percent). Although average revenue was fairly high and even increased in 1970, it did not increase enough to offset the high and increasing average transaction and financial costs because NACF's nonearning assets, such as accounts receivable, advance payments, and inventory accounted for as much as 35 percent in total assets in both years. Moreover, they also increased in absolute value in 1970 (Table 34).

Clearly, net margins of an RFI such as NACF are dependent on a number of complex and interrelated factors, not just interest rates. There is a need for reforms of factors related to nonprice and deposit rates.

---

[26]Brake (1971) recommended that the finance and credit and insurance operations should ultimately become separate institutions from the NACF.

[27]Even in 1975 and 1976 this institution merely broke even with unit net margins at barely 0.0003 and 0.0004 percent, respectively, computed from the data given in Korea, Republic of, NACF (various years).

[28]This is consistent with the earlier observation about interest rate inelasticity of deposits, which is discussed in empirical terms for the Republic of Korea as well as some other developing countries in Chapter 7.

Table 33—Transaction and financial costs and net margin of the National Agricultural Cooperative Federation, Republic of Korea, 1967 and 1970

Variable in Real Terms[a]	1967	1970	Increase in 1970
		(percent)	
Unit transaction costs[b]	5.89	6.68	13.4
Unit financial costs[b]	2.40	2.90	20.8
Unit revenue[b]	7.73	7.98	16.2
Unit net margin[b]	-0.56	-0.60	-7.1

Source: Brake 1971.
[a]Real terms are derived by applying the agricultural GDP deflator with a base year of 1975.
[b]Computed as a percentage of all assets plus liabilities.

County Cooperatives, Republic of Korea

The county cooperatives in Korea are major contact points for farmers (Brake 1971; Korea, Republic of, NACF various years). Over time, their number and accessibility have improved. Their sources of funds include borrowings, deposits, and some equity capital. These cooperatives seem to have succeeded in mobilizing deposits, achieving lower average transaction costs, as well as viability. However, the preceding discussion on high unit financial costs and the holding of large amounts of nonearning

Table 34—Structure of assets and liabilities of the National Agricultural Cooperative Federation, Republic of Korea, 1967 and 1970

Liabilities in Real Terms[a]	1967 Value	1967 Percent	1970 Value	1970 Percent
	(W million)		(W million)	
Credit and banking				
Deposits from county cooperatives	60,927	18.3	49,531	10.9
Deposits from public	23,300	7.0	19,844	4.4
Borrowings	198,423	59.6	310,512	68.3
Miscellaneous	24,382	7.3	14,210	3.1
Subtotal	307,032	92.2	394,097	86.7
Mutual insurance	8,887	2.7	24,705	5.4
Business				
Payables and advance receipts	6,177	1.8	17,475	3.8
Liabilities on consignment	2,464	. . .	1,846	. . .
Miscellaneous	4,168	3.0	9,311	2.0
Subtotal	12,809	3.0	28,732	5.8
Total assets	333,172	98.3	454,716	99.5

Source: Brake 1971.
Note: Columns may not add to 100 due to rounding. The ellipses (. . .) indicate a nil or negligible amount.
[a]Real terms are derived by applying the agricultural GDP deflator with a base of 1975.

assets applies to them too. Otherwise these cooperatives would have enjoyed lower unit transaction costs, lower unit financial costs, and larger scale economies, in addition to greater viability. Thus, these internal and external constraints need reform.

In 1970, there were 130 county cooperatives; by the mid-1970s, their number had increased to 150, with almost all cooperatives having at least one branch. Their sources of funds are borrowings, deposits, and some equity. Their activities include credit, insurance, purchasing, marketing, and processing, though the first two dominate. The credit-deposit ratio of county cooperatives was 1.02 in 1967 and 1.20 in 1970.

In both 1967 and 1970, these cooperatives had positive net margins. However, the average net margin declined to 0.07 percent in 1970, compared with 0.23 percent in 1967, despite a decrease in unit transaction costs in 1970 (Table 35). The lower net margin in 1970 was, therefore, mainly the result of a substantial increase in unit financial costs, which was due to an increase in interest rates on deposits as well as an increase in deposit balances,[29] and a moderate increase in unit revenue (Table 35). The increase in revenues again is the result of fairly large increases in nonearning assets such as accounts receivables, advance payments, and inventories (Table 36). If the county cooperatives had managed these assets better and the interest rates on deposits had not risen, their net margins would have been much better.

Primary Cooperatives, Republic of Korea

These cooperatives are the ultimate and most proximate link to farmers (Brake 1971; Korea, Republic of, NACF various years). Over time, they have been reorganized by merger, as they were considered too small. By

Table 35—Transaction and financial costs and net margin of the county/city cooperatives, Republic of Korea, 1967 and 1970

Variable in Real Terms[a]	1967	1970	Increase in 1970
		(percent)	
Unit transaction costs[b]	5.47	4.06	25.8
Unit financial costs[b]	1.79	3.38	88.8
Unit revenue[b]	7.49	8.51	13.6
Unit net margin[b]	0.23	0.07	−69.6

Source: Brake 1971; and Korea, Republic of, NACF, various years.
[a]Real terms are derived by applying the agricultural GDP deflator with a base year of 1975.
[b]Computed as a percentage of all assets plus liabilities.

[29]This increase in financial costs may have resulted largely from the better accessibility to the rural populace afforded by the widespread network of county cooperatives and their branches. This is consistent with the finding on interest inelasticity of deposits.

Table 36—Structure of assets and liabilities of the county/city cooperatives, Republic of Korea, 1967 and 1970

Assets and Liabilities in Real Terms[a]	1967		1970	
	Value	Percent	Value	Percent
	(W million)		(W million)	
Assets				
Credit and banking				
Cash on hand and in bank	83,286	27.8	81,091	16.0
Loans	104,554	34.8	284,003	56.1
Miscellaneous, including securities	7,483	2.5	5,863	1.2
Subtotal	195,323	65.1	370,957	73.3
Mutual insurance	390	. . .	5,700	1.1
Trading and marketing				
Accounts receivable	42,098	14.0	37,890	7.5
Payments in advance	399	. . .	1,051	. . .
Credit on consignment	1,211	. . .	303	. . .
Inventory	42,882	14.3	57,987	11.5
Miscellaneous	6,659	2.2	11,697	2.3
Subtotal	93,249	30.5	108,928	21.3
Fixed assets	11,044	3.7	19,732	3.9
Total assets	300,006	99.3	505,830	99.6
Liabilities				
Credit and banking				
Deposits	102,943	34.3	235,965	46.6
Advance from government	26,180	8.7	44,078	8.7
Loans from government	30,199	10.1	31,676	6.3
Agricultural credit debentures	8,159	2.7	4,078	. . .
Borrowed irrigation funds from government	39,643	13.2	34,595	6.8
Miscellaneous	3,435	1.1	6,777	1.3
Subtotal	210,559	70.1	357,169	69.7
Insurance	798	. . .	5,422	1.1
Trading and marketing				
Accounts payable	77,108	25.7	81,949	16.2
Receipts in advance	354	. . .	332	. . .
Payables on consignment	379	. . .	105	. . .
Miscellaneous liabilities	4,330	1.4	46,370	9.1
Subtotal	82,171	27.1	128,756	25.3
Other liabilities (including paid-up capital, reserves, and net profit)	6,778	2.3	14,483	2.9
Total liabilities	300,006	99.5	505,830	99.0

Source: Brake 1971.
Note: Columns may not add to 100 due to rounding. The ellipses (. . .) indicate a nil or negligible amount.
[a]Real terms are derived by applying the agricultural GDP deflator with a base of 1975.

the mid-1970s, they covered 80 percent of the Republic of Korea's farm households.

Their sources of funds are the same as those for federations, but they are truly multifunctional, which has greatly facilitated agricultural growth and achieved net margins in areas as diverse as single-crop paddy, double-crop paddy, and upland plantings. Their net margins could have been even better had they not been functioning under the high interest rate structure described earlier.

Primary cooperatives are organized at the township level, although originally a high proportion of them were in villages. In 1965, they were reorganized because the primaries located in villages were small institutions with small scales of operation. They numbered 18,000 with an average membership of only 125. After 1965, many of them merged, and the number was reduced to 5,859 in 1970, with an average membership of 379. By the mid-1970s, the average membership per primary was 1,217.

The main sources of funds of these primary cooperatives are borrowings, deposits, and equity. Moreover, they are multipurpose cooperatives not only in design, but also in practice. They extend credit, market produce, supply farm inputs, and provide deposit services. Because data are unavailable on the relative share of each of these functions, this aspect cannot be analyzed. However, Brake (1971) estimates that farm input supply accounted for the largest share (49 percent), followed by farm produce marketing (39 percent), and credit and deposit services accounted for the remaining 12 percent. The lower figure for credit and deposit facilities could be due to some farm inputs sold on credit and some farm produce collected in the form of deposits in the marketing operations. Nevertheless, the multifunctional structure of primary cooperatives has greatly facilitated agricultural growth and the viability of these institutions.

These primary cooperatives have positive net margins, as seen in Table 37, which shows the relevant data for primaries located in single-crop paddy, double-crop paddy, and upland areas. Moreover, the unit net margin in 1970 was lowest in the single-crop paddy area, followed by the double-crop paddy area, and then the upland area. Barely 7 percent of all primary cooperatives reported losses for 1970.

It is worth recalling that these primary cooperatives also functioned under the interest rate policy discussed earlier. If rates on deposits had not been raised substantially, the cooperatives could probably have improved their viability, but this could not be examined fully because detailed data were not available.

Table 37—Data on viability of primary cooperatives, by crop area, Republic of Korea, 1970

Area	Number of Primaries	Unit Net Margin[a]	Cooperatives Reporting Losses
		(percent)	
Single-crop paddy	1,389	0.43	6
Double-crop paddy	3,634	0.54	7
Upland	836	0.74	9
All areas	5,859	0.55	7

Source: Brake 1971; Korea, Republic of, NACF various years.
[a]Computed as a percentage of all assets plus liabilities.

6

Response of Rural Loan Demand to Interest Rates and Nonprice Determinants

I n this chapter, factors influencing demand for farm-level loans and the response of this demand to interest rates are analyzed. Implications are drawn for interest rate policy and the effects of scale on RFIs and their contributions to agricultural development. There are three reasons for undertaking this analysis. First, available studies examine the first of these two objectives but generally do not bring out the empirical results on the relative importance of various factors and the elasticity of the demand for rural loans with respect to the real interest rate. Second, the bulk of the interpretive literature implicitly assumes that interest rate is the prime determinant of demand and that its impact on rural loan demand is inelastic. And third, this literature does not consider how the level of interest rates can adversely affect scale economies in transaction costs of RFIs and their contributions to agricultural development.

Factors Influencing Rural Loan Demand

There are only seven studies that examine this issue quantitatively (Pani 1966; Long 1968; Araujo 1967; Paulson 1984; Nyanin 1969; Hesser and Schuh 1962; and Lins 1972).[30] These studies provide 14 cases—4 in India, 3 in Kenya, 5 in the United States, and 1 each in Brazil and the Republic of Korea (Tables 38, 39, 40). All except one use single-equation ordinary least squares as the technique of estimation. The one exception uses two-stage least squares with an instrumental variable technique to estimate the reduced form of equation. Single-equation models may be preponderant because their data requirements are less demanding, or because they do not require the assumption of spontaneous adjustments

---

[30]One study on India (Iqbal 1982) is excluded from detailed analysis because it examines the influence of the nominal instead of the real interest rate. However, Iqbal's study finds that noninterest factors like transitory income, technology (expectations about profitable investment opportunities), family size, and owned land have greater influence than the nominal interest rate. Moreover, it shows that the response of rural borrowings to the nominal interest rate is elastic, with an interest rate elasticity of –1.4 percent.

Table 38—Estimated multivariate models of demand for rural credit in India, a low-income country

	Pani 1966		Long 1968	
Item	CI + NIL 1951/52	CI + NIL 1956/57	CI + NIL 1951/52	I + NILOS 1951/52
Real interest rate	−4.43 (−2.4)*[2]	−4.04 (−1.4)***[3]	−16.0 (−1.1)*[5]	−5.9 (−2.6)*[5]
Value of investment	0.74 (5.3)*[1]	0.63 (2.86)*[1]	0.59 (18.4)*[1]	0.53 (11.1)*[1]
Family expenditure	0.16 (1.8)***[3]	0.22 (1.5)***[2]	0.11 (3.0)*[4]	0.20 (3.7)*[4]
Transitory income	...	...	0.64 (0.5)[6]	−0.11 (−1.2)[6]
Assets	0.004 (1.0)[4]	0.001 (0.20)[4]	0.01 (3.8)*[3]	0.02 (5.4)*[2]
Assets squared	...	...	-0.86×10^{-7} (−4.8)*[2]	-0.14×10^{-6} (−5.2)*[3]
$\bar{R}^2$	0.77	0.84	0.52	0.39
Number of farms	75	36	672	672

Sources: Pani 1966; Long 1968.

Notes: CI+NIL = Current institutional plus noninstitutional loans;
           I+NILOS = Institutional plus noninstitutional loans outstanding.

   The figures in parentheses are t-values. The figures in brackets are ranks based on the size of the t-values (ignoring signs). See Appendix 1 for the proof showing that the ranks would be the same based on t-values and standardized beta.

   *Significant at 1 percent.
  **Significant at 5 percent.
 ***Significant at 10 percent.

implied in simultaneous systems. Moreover, such an assumption does not hold, as the rural financial market is imperfect by definition.

Only the studies on India measure rural loan demand as farm-level institutional plus noninstitutional loans. All the remaining studies define rural loan demand as farm-level institutional loans only. All of the studies, except those on Kenya and the United States, utilize cross-section data for a year or two. The Kenyan study uses cross-section data combined with quarterly time series data, whereas the studies on the United States use fairly long annual time series. Six more studies qualitatively deal with the noninterest factors, though some of them also analyze quantitatively the response of the rural loan demand to the real interest rate. Some of the six argue that accessibility to RFIs is a more important determinant than the interest rate.

The specified models in the three tables explain large amounts of variation in rural loan demand. Most have the expected negative sign for

Table 39—Estimated multivariate models of demand for rural credit in three middle-income countries

Item	Brazil 1965[a] CIL	Kenya CCBL 1977-83[b] Model I	Model II	Model III	Republic of Korea 1970[c] CIL
Real interest rate	-22.32 (0.2)[6]	-0.41 (1.7)[3]	-0.39 (-1.6)[8]	-0.46 (-1.9)***[4]	...
Value of investment	-0.22 (4.3)*[2]	...	...	...	0.93
Net cash farm income	-0.18 (-4.1)*[3]	...	...	...	...
Cash at beginning year	...	...	...	...	-0.02
Debt outstanding	-0.85 (3.2)*[4]	...	...	...	0.58
Ratio of debt outstanding to value of assets	-268.26 (-2.7)*[5]	...	...	...	...
Years of schooling	604.60 (11.8)*[1]	...	...	...	...
AFC lending rate to bank lending rate	...	1.39 (1.1)[11]	1.74 (1.4)[9]	1.11 (0.9)[9]	...
Amount of AFC loan approvals during the quarter weighted by the probability that there was quantity rationing	...	-0.002 (-0.6)[16]	-0.001 (-0.5)[12]	-0.001 (-0.5)[10]	...
Amount of AFC credit approved in the previous quarters weighted by the probability that there was credit rationing in the previous quarter	...	-0.003 (-0.9)[12]	-0.001 (-0.5)[13]	-0.001 (-0.3)[11]	...
Time trend	...	2.07 (0.7)[15]	0.27 (3.5)*[1]	0.24 (3.0)*[2]	...
Per capita GNP	...	-13.23 (-1.9)[2]	-11.90 (2.8)*[3]	-11.41 (-2.8)*[3]	...
Percent of population that has wage employment in the area	...	2.79 (2.5)*[1]	3.29 (3.4)*[2]	3.14 (3.2)*[1]	...
Percent of trust land in the area that has been adjudicated and registered	...	0.55 (0.8)[14]	...	...	...
Prices					
Inputs	...	-47.35 (-1.2)[8]	-1.58 (-2.7)*[4]	...	...
Coffee	...	-28.80 (-1.1)[10]	0.33 (1.1)[11]		

(continued)

Table 39—Continued

Item	Brazil 1965[a] CIL	Kenya CCBL 1977-83[b] Model I	Model II	Model III	Republic of Korea 1970[c] CIL
Prices, continued					
Wheat	...	−48.40 (−0.5)[17]	...	...	...
Tea	...	40.26 (1.4)[4]	...	...	...
Milk	...	−49.08 (−1.3)[5]	...	...	...
Sugar	...	43.31 (1.2)[9]	...	...	...
Beef	...	1.05 (0.2)[19]	...	...	...
Maize	...	3.12 (0.1)[20]	...	...	...
Region					
Kakamega	...	1.92 (1.3)[6]	2.28 (1.6)[7]	2.07 (1.5)[7]	...
Eldoret	...	0.62 (1.3)[7]	0.47 (1.1)[10]	0.42 (0.9)[8]	...
Embu	...	1.24 (0.8)[13]	2.06 (1.7)**[6]	1.89 (1.6)[6]	...
Machakos	...	1.24 (0.4)[18]	3.34 (2.0)**[5]	3.09 (1.8)[5]	...
$\bar{R}^2$	0.74	0.73	0.76	0.74	0.22
Number of farms/ observations	132	28	28	28	438

Notes: CIL is current institutional loans. CCBL is current commercial bank loans. AFC is Agricultural Finance Corporation. The figures in parentheses are t-values. The figures in brackets are ranks based on the size of the t-values (ignoring signs). See Appendix 1 for the proof showing that the ranks would be the same based on t-values and standardized beta.

[a]Araujo 1967.
[b]Penny 1968.
[c]Nyanin 1969.
*Significant at 1 percent.
**Significant at 5 percent.
***Significant at 10 percent.

the coefficient associated with the real interest rate, but only 7 of the 14 are statistically significant. A large majority of the coefficients associated with the factors related to the noninterest rate have expected signs and are statistically significant. Major exceptions are the three models on Kenya in which the majority of the coefficients related to both the interest and noninterest rate factors are statistically insignificant or less significant (Table 39).

Table 40—Estimated multivariate models of demand for rural
credit in the United States, a high-income country

Item	Hesser and Schuh 1962, 1927-59 GCFMIL	Lins 1972, 1947-69			
		NCIL Land Banks	NCIL Commercial Banks	NCIL Insurance Company	NCIL Others
Real interest rate	−0.90 (−1.8)**[5]	−3.53 (−0.1)[4]	3.35 (0.1)[4]	−337.23 (−4.78)*[2]	−17.37 (−0.1)[4]
Internal funds	−1.99 (−2.6)*[4]	...	...	...	...
Money balance/gross farm expenses	...	−17.01 (−2.5)*[1]	−4.75 (−0.7)[3]	−36.93 (−5.2)*[1]	−20.00 (−1.6)**[2]
Technology	−3.36 (−2.9)*[3]	...	...	...	...
Wage rate	0.91 (3.1)*[2]	...	...	...	...
Net capital appreciation	...	5.05 (0.7)[3]	7.14 (1.32)[2]	3.99 (0.7)[4]	20.45 (2.1)*[1]
Net farm and nonfarm income	...	19.84 (2.0)*[2]	11.29 (1.34)[1]	22.28 (2.4)*[3]	16.09 (1.0)[3]
Lagged dependent variable	0.86 (3.7)*[1]	...	...	...	...
$\bar{R}^2$	0.66	0.83	0.64	0.71	0.82
Number of observations	33	23	23	23	23

Sources: Hesser and Schuh 1962; Lins 1972.

Notes: GCFMIL = Gross current farm mortgage institutional loans;
NCIL   = Net current institutional loans.

The figures in parentheses are t-values. The figures in brackets are ranks based on the size of the t-values (ignoring signs). See Appendix 1 for the proof showing that the ranks would be the same based on t-values and standardized beta.

*Significant at 1 percent.
**Significant at 5 percent.

These studies further show that real interest rate is a relatively less important variable than other factors in influencing demand for rural credit in both developing and developed countries. But the real interest rate is a more important determinant in LICs than in MICs or HICs. Although this result may to some extent have been influenced by the lack of uniformity in noninterest rate factors covered in various studies, it may still be considered quite reliable. This is because the percentage of variation in rural loan demand explained by the selected independent variables (R^2) in studies on LICs is comparable to that in studies on MICs and HICs. It may also be because rural loan demand in studies on LICs includes both institutional and noninstitutional loans. Moreover, interest rates on noninstitutional loans are high. For these reasons, it is instructive to identify the relative importance of various factors influencing demand for farm-level loans. This is derived by ranking these factors based on the magnitude of their *t*-values, ignoring signs (see the bracketed figures under the regression coefficients in Tables 38, 39, and 40). Before these results are analyzed, it should be noted that the relative ranking of explanatory factors based on this method is the same as that based on standardized beta. Appendix 1 gives proof of this.

Unlike the United States, the most important determinant of demand for rural loans in developing countries is the adoption of new technology (investment expenditure). This is true of countries as widely different as Brazil, India, and the Republic of Korea. For the Republic of Korea and Brazil, it holds for as late as the mid- to late-1960s (Table 39). Other factors, in order of importance for LICs, are risk-bearing ability and availability of internal finance. In MICs, they are per capita GNP, time trend, wage employment, input prices, output prices, and credit quotas. And in the HICs, they are expectations about the availability of credit (as indicated by loans available in the last year), wage rate (a proxy for increased need for credit), technology (as measured by changes in output per unit of total inputs, that is, the incremental output-input ratio), and internal finance.

With the exception of the real interest rate, internal finance availability, and past debt, all other variables have a positive effect on rural loan demand. These assumed signs of the coefficients associated with various determinants hold empirically in all data except those for the United States, where signs of coefficients associated with some explanatory factors are not according to expectations. These factors are technological change in the model for farm mortgage loans (Hesser and Schuh 1962), the ratio of money balances to gross farm expenses in the model for land bank credit (Lins 1972), and interest rate in the model for commercial bank loans (Lins 1972). Unexpected signs for the last two of these three variables may not be viewed with great concern, as the coefficients are statistically insignificant.

The negative sign of the coefficient associated with the technological change variable in the model on farm mortgage loans is explained in Hesser and Schuh 1962, which suggests that there are two types of substitution effects of technological change on the demand for farm mortgage credit. One of these leads to the increase in this demand, because capital is being substituted for labor on account of the basic nature of mechanical technological change. The other leads to the decrease in loan demand, because labor is substituted for capital due to the decline in price of labor relative to the price of capital. The negative coefficient of the estimated model implies that this latter substitution effect has more than outweighed the former, holding other factors constant. However, this explanation needs further probing for two reasons. First, the negative substitution effect attributed to a decline in the price of labor relative to the price of capital is not factually correct. The period covered by this model did not witness a decline in relative factor prices. In fact, they increased. Another reason to question the explanation is that the model also considers real wage rate as one of the separate determinants of demand for credit. This variable has a positive coefficient, which is explained by Hesser and Schuh (1962) on the grounds that, as real wage rate increases, holding other factors constant, capital is substituted for labor and hence the loan demand increases. It appears that Hesser and Schuh now contend that the effect of capital substitution for labor is more powerful than what is argued earlier.

These intertwined substitution effects could have been sorted out better if the ratio of wage rate to the price of capital, instead of the ratio of wage rate to the price of consumer goods, had been used in the model to capture the two substitution effects in net terms, as well as the net effect of technological change proper. Under such a specification, signs of both the variables should be positive. This is because when the price of labor relative to that of capital increases, loan demand would also increase. Similarly, when technological change occurs, the demand for loans would invariably increase because adoption of this change usually requires higher investment. If, in this situation, the interest rate on rural loans is raised, then it would adversely affect investment and hence adoption of new technology. Consequently, the contribution of RFIs to agricultural development would be reduced. This is in addition to adverse implications for the RFIs' viability through reduction in their scales of operation, which could lead to scale diseconomies for them. This will especially hold true in LICs, where loan demand is interest-elastic and much higher.

Response of Rural Loan Demand to the Interest Rate

In addition to the 14 discussed above, 17 more cases are considered here. Out of a total of 31 cases, 15 show that the rural loan demand is highly elastic to the real interest rate, 3 that it is moderately elastic (Table 41), and 4 that it is slightly elastic. Only 9 cases indicate that demand is interest-inelastic.

Three of the nine inelastic examples are for U.S. agriculture; the remaining six are for Brazil, India, Indonesia, Mexico, and Sudan. The results for these five countries are based on normative models from which a derived demand schedule for loans is constructed. These are drawn from a standard static linear programming framework or from a profit function approach. Both these frameworks are inflexible to account for the wide variety of constraints that operate on the maximization of profits by farmers. They, therefore, may not provide a realistic estimation of loan demand response to the interest rate.[31] The 18 cases that show high-to-moderate elasticity of demand for rural loans with respect to the real interest rate appear to be more realistic, as they are based either on positive loan demand models or on normative models derived from risk or recursive programming frameworks.

---

[31]Hence, in further analysis, these elasticity estimates are not considered.

Table 41—Evidence on interest elasticity of demand for rural loans in selected developing and developed countries

Type of Demand, Region, Country, Income Group, Study Period, Source	Range of Interest Elasticity					Overall Average
	More than -0.70	-0.39 to -0.70	-0.21 to -0.38	-0.10 to -0.20	Less than -0.10	
Institutional loans						
Sub-Saharan Africa						
Low-income country						
Kenya, 1977-83 (Paulson 1984)	...	-0.39 to -0.46[a]	...	...	...	-0.43[a]
Simple average	...	-0.39 to -0.46	...	...	...	-0.43
Asia						
Low-income countries						
Bangladesh, 1962/63 (Adams 1979)	-1.98[b]	...	...	...	...	-1.98[b]
India, 1967/68 (Tyagi and Pandey 1982)	...	...	...	...	-0.006 to -0.029[c]	-0.02[c]
India, mid-1970s (Kumar, Joshi, and Murlidharan 1978)	...	...	-0.25 to 0.35[c]	...	...	-0.30[c]
India, 1978/79 (Tyagi and Pandey 1982)	-1.64 to -4.52[c] Medium-size, mechanized farms	-0.50 to -0.69[c] Large-size, partially mechanized farms	-0.24 to -0.25[c] Bullock-operated farms	...	...	-1.31[c]
India, 1986/87 (Agricultural Finance Corporation 1988)	-0.90[d]	...	...	...	...	-0.90[d]
India, commercial banks, 1986/87 (Agricultural Finance Corporation 1988)	-1.37[d]	...	...	...	...	-1.37[d]

(continued)

Table 41—Continued

Type of Demand, Region, Country, Income Group, Study Period, Source	Range of Interest Elasticity					Overall Average
	More than -0.70	-0.39 to -0.70	-0.21 to -0.38	-0.10 to -0.20	Less than -0.10	
India, PACS, 1986/87 (Agricultural Finance Corporation 1988)	-1.12[d]	…	…	…	…	-1.12[d]
Indonesia, late 1960s (Hadiwegeno 1974)				e		e
Simple average, early 1960s	-1.98	…	…	…	…	-1.98
Simple average, late 1960s	…	…	…	e	…	-0.02
Simple average, mid-1970s	…	…	…	…	-0.006 to -0.029	-0.30
Simple average, late 1970s	-1.64 to -4.52	-0.50 to -0.69	-0.25 to -0.35	…	…	-1.31
Simple average, mid-1980s	-1.25	…	-0.24 to -0.25	…	…	-1.25
Near East and Mediterranean Basin						
Low-income country						
Sudan, Gazira Scheme, late-1960s, (S. El-M. Ahmed 1977)	…	…	…	e	…	e
Simple average	…	…	…	e	…	e
Latin America and the Caribbean						
Middle-income countries						
Brazil, 1960 (Singh 1970)	-1.75[f]	…	…	…	…	-1.75[f]
Brazil, 1965 (Araujo 1967)	…	…	…	…	-0.084[e]	-0.08[e]
Brazil, 1969 (Nehman 1973)	…	…	…	…	-0.0001[e]	-0.0001[e]
Brazil, 1971 (Adams 1979)	-1.83[b]	…	…	…	…	-1.83[b]
Brazil, 1971-72 (Peres 1976)	g	…	…	…	…	g
Mexico, 1966 (Kumar, Joshi, and Murlidharan 1978)	…	…	…	-0.111[e]	…	-0.11[e]
Simple average, 1960s	-1.75	…	…	…	…	-1.75
Simple average, mid-1960s	…	…	…	-0.111	-0.084	-0.98

(continued)

Table 41—Continued

Type of Demand, Region, Country, Income Group, Study Period, Source	Range of Interest Elasticity					Overall Average
	More than -0.70	-0.39 to -0.70	-0.21 to -0.38	-0.10 to -0.20	Less than -0.10	
Simple average, late 1960s and early 1970s	-1.83	...	...	...	-0.001	-0.92
North America						
High-income country						
United States, 1921-59 (Hesser and Schuh 1962)	-2.29[h]	...	...	...	...	-2.29[h]
United States, 1947-69 (insurance loans) (Lins 1972)	-8.37[i]	...	...	...	...	-8.37[i]
United States, 1947-67 (commercial bank loans) (Lins 1972)	...	...	...	Inelastic[i]	...	Inelastic[i]
United States, 1947-69 (land bank loans) (Lins 1972)	...	...	...	Inelastic[i]	...	Inelastic[i]
United States, 1947-69 (other institutional loans) (Lins 1972)	...	...	...	Inelastic[i]	...	Inelastic[i]
Simple average of last three because they are comparable with other countries	...	...	...	Inelastic	...	Inelastic
Institutional and noninstitutional loans						
Asia						
Low-income countries						
India, outstanding loans, 1951/52 (Long 1968)	-1.34[i]	...	...	...	...	-1.34[i]
India, current loans, 1951/52 (Long 1968)	...	...	-0.25[i]	...	...	-0.25[i]
India, current loans, 1951/52 (Long 1968)	...	-0.43[i]	...	...	...	-0.43[i]

(continued)

Table 41—Continued

Type of Demand, Region, Country, Income Group, Study Period, Source	Range of Interest Elasticity					Overall Average
	More than -0.70	-0.39 to -0.70	-0.21 to -0.38	-0.10 to -0.20	Less than -0.10	
India, current loans, 1956/57 (Long 1968)	...	...	-0.25[i]	...	...	-0.25[i]
Indian Punjab, 1955, 1965, 1970, and 1980 (Day and Singh 1977)	g	...	...	...	...	g
India, 1986/87 (Agricultural Finance Corporation 1988)	-1.11	...	...	...	...	-1.11[d]
Nepal, late 1960s (Jha 1978)	-1.84	...	...	...	...	1.84
Simple average, early 1950s	-1.34[i]	-0.43[i]	-0.25[i]	...	...	-0.67[i]
Simple average, mid-1950s	g	...	-0.25[i]	...	...	g
Simple average, mid-1960s	g	...	...	...	...	g
Simple average, late 1960s	-1.84	...	...	...	...	-1.84
Simple average, mid-1980s	-1.11	...	...	...	...	-1.11

Notes: PACS are primary agricultural credit societies.

[a] Derived by the authors on the basis of descriptive economic analysis of data.

[b] Elasticities at the mean level with respect to the effective price of borrowing (interest plus noninterest costs of borrowing).

[c] Based on normative loan demand models utilizing the Cobb-Douglas production function and profit function approach.

[d] Estimated on the basis of a positive simple loan demand model utilizing a semi-log functional form, wherein the dependent variable is in log form, while the independent variable (interest rate) is in linear form. This functional form is used because its estimation gives higher R^2 and F values.

[e] Based on normatively derived loan demand models utilizing a standard linear programming framework.

[f] Based on normatively derived loan demand models utilizing a dynamic programming framework.

[g] Based on normatively derived loan demand models utilizing a recursive programming framework.

[h] Based on positive loan demand and supply models utilizing a simultaneous equation framework.

[i] Based on positive multivariate loan demand models utilizing a Cobb-Douglas function.

The interest elasticity of demand for rural credit is highest in LICs (–0.25 to –1.98 with an average of –1.31) followed by MICs (–0.43 to –1.83 with an average of –1.10), and HICs (0 to –2.29) (Table 41). Lower elasticity in LICs is for farmers with traditional technology, but this does not hold for farmers with new technology. Both in Brazil and India, this elasticity is becoming more elastic over time. In India, it increased from –0.79 in the 1950s to –1.30 in the 1970s to –1.37 in the mid-1980s. In Brazil, it increased from –1.75 in 1960 to –1.83 in 1971. This is perhaps because of the increased burden of interest costs on account of the larger credit requirement and the increased interest rates on loans. Moreover, in India, interest elasticity of demand for rural loans by medium-sized farms mechanized for irrigation is higher (–1.64 to –4.52) than that for farms with traditional technology (–0.24 to –0.25). But, in the United States, this elasticity is becoming more inelastic over time (–2.29 during 1921-59 to almost zero during 1947-69). This may be because U.S. agriculture had fully transformed technologically by that time. It may already have achieved critical minimum growth. Hence, U.S. farmers may have been able to finance relatively more from internal sources. These explanations appear consistent with the higher interest elasticity of rural deposits in the United States than in LICs and MICs, as will be shown in the next chapter.

Recursive programming studies on the Indian Punjab (Day and Singh 1977) and Brazil (Peres 1976), where agriculture is not fully transformed technologically, show that, over time as agriculture becomes more commercialized and more intimately linked with the markets for new inputs and for surplus production, the interest elasticity of demand for rural credit increases. These studies, however, also show that this elasticity is higher for larger farmers than for smaller ones. This result may have been influenced by the fact that these studies typically consider only working capital credit for meeting farm input expenses. But a risk programming model for a cross-section of sample farmers in Brazil (Peres 1976) shows that small farmers' demand for rural loans is more interest-elastic than the large farmers' demand for such loans. Moreover, it shows that this demand becomes even more interest-elastic for small farmers when family labor is rightly considered as a variable instead of as a fixed factor, with corresponding cash outlay to pay for it. The case for large farmers is similar when the constraint on labor availability is introduced.

Only 4 of the 22 studies under review provide relevant data to compute interest elasticity of demand for rural credit by different-sized farms. A study on Brazil (Adams 1979) shows that this elasticity is higher for large farmers (–2.33) than for medium farmers (–1.33) (Table 42). But two studies on India (Agricultural Finance Corporation 1988; Pani 1966), and one on Nepal (Jha 1978), also presented in Table 42, show that this elasticity is higher for smaller farmers, including landless laborers and medium-sized farms (–0.25 to –3.35) than for larger farms (–0.15 to –2.04). The two studies on India also show that over time the interest elasticity of demand for rural credit for the poorer farm people is increasing (–0.10 to –2.04), whereas that for the richer is weakening (–0.51 to –0.24).

Table 42—Evidence on interest elasticity of demand for rural loans by farm size or income group in selected developing countries

Farm Size or Income Group	Brazil Mid-1960s[a] (by Farm Size, CIL) (Adams 1979)	India 1951/52[b] (by Income Group, CIL and CNIL) (Pani 1966)	India 1956/57[c] (by Income Group, CIL and CNIL) (Pani 1966)	India 1986/87[d] (by Farm Size, ILO) (Agricultural Finance Corporation 1988)	Nepal Late 1960s[e] (by Farm Size, CIL and CNIL) (Jha 1978)
Landless (50 percent)/low-income (30 percent)	...	-0.10	-0.25	-0.71	...
Marginal/middle-income (40 percent)	...	...	-0.39	-2.04	...
Small/high-income (30 percent)	...	...	-0.10	-0.71	-3.35
Medium	-1.33	...	...	...	-136.16
Large (50 percent)/high-income (10 percent)	-2.33	-0.51	-0.15	-0.24	-2.04
Simple average	-1.83	-0.31	-0.22	-0.93[f] (-1.15)	-47.18[g] (-2.78)

Notes: CIL is current institutional loans, CNIL is current noninstitutional loans, and ILO is institutional loans outstanding.

[a] Arc elasticities are estimated from group data for a small sample of 150 farmers. These elasticities are with respect to total unit costs of borrowing, including interest and noninterest costs of borrowing. Medium farm size is 49.41-113.50 acres and large size is greater than 113.50 acres.

[b] Based on a multivariate double-log loan demand model based on large-scale nationwide sample survey data. In this column elasticities are for two groups of income deciles, namely, bottom 50 percent and top 50 percent.

[c] Same as note b above except that the elasticities are for four income decile groups, namely, bottom 30 percent, middle 40 percent, top 30 percent, and top 10 percent.

[d] Estimated at the mean level on the basis of a simple semilog loan demand model based on large-scale nationwide sample survey data. These mean elasticities are for landless, marginal (up to 2.5 acres), small (2.51 to 5 acres), and large (above 5 acres) farm sizes.

[e] These are also arc elasticities estimated from group data for a small sample of 142 farmers in the Tarai region of Nepal. Small-farm size is defined as less than 10 acres, medium-size as 10 to 17 acres, and large as 17 to 29 acres.

[f] The figure in parentheses is a simple average computed after excluding large farms.

[g] The figure in parentheses is a simple average computed after excluding medium-size farms.

Findings of this and the preceding chapters are used to develop Table 43 on the comparative static impact of increasing the interest rate on rural loans on demand for these loans, and consequently on scale economies in transaction costs of RFIs in LICs. Based on the findings of this study, it is assumed that an average of the elasticity of rural loan demand with respect to the real interest rate is –1.31, and that the scale parameter for transaction costs is 0.83. Thus, when the interest rate is increased by 10 percent, rural loan demand would decrease by 13.1 percent, and the RFIs would then suffer from diseconomies of scale in their transaction costs, as the scale parameter increases to 1.05.

To conclude, raising lending rates when agriculture is in the process of transformation has distinctly negative implications for scale economies and hence for the level of transaction costs of RFIs, as well as for agricultural development.

Table 43—Impact of raising the interest rate on farm-level loans and on scale economies in transaction costs of rural financial institutions (RFIs) in low-income countries

Real Interest Rate on Farm-Level Loans	Demand for Farm-Level Loans at a Given Lending Rate	Volume of Business at a Given Lending Rate	Scale Parameter for Transaction Costs of RFIs
(percent/year)	(Rs)		(ratio)
2.00	100.00	200.00	0.83
2.20	86.90[a]	173.80[b]	1.05[c]

[a]A 10 percent increase in the lending rate from 2.0 to 2.2 would reduce demand for farm-level loans by 13.1 percent because the interest rate elasticity of these loans is 1.31 percent.
[b]In order to lend Rs 86.90, an RFI would have to borrow Rs 86.90. Thus, its volume of business (loans plus borrowings) would be Rs 173.80. It is necessary to derive this figure because transaction costs of RFIs are common for loans and borrowings.
[c]The scale parameter for these costs was 0.83 prior to an upward revision in the lending rate. It now becomes 1.05, as the volume of business has declined by 26.2 percent. In other words, after the upward revision in the lending rate, the scale parameter would

7

Response of Supply of Rural Deposits to Interest Rate and Nonprice Variables

In this chapter, factors are analyzed that influence the supply of deposits by the farm sector. The response of these deposits to real interest rates is also examined. Based on these findings, inferences for institutional rural finance policy are drawn.

A significant number of studies do not make a distinction between the financial and nonfinancial forms in which rural households hold their savings. Some studies covered in this chapter therefore overlap with those covered in the next chapter on response of supply of rural savings to interest rate and nonprice determinants.

How farm households save is important because, during the agricultural transformation phase, farmers prefer to hold savings in the form of modern physical productive resources, rather than in financial savings. These resources provide capital formation in new forms that enable them to improve their productivity and incomes. This distinction is analytically important because the impact of the interest rate on rural deposits is expected to be positive and that on overall savings (physical plus financial) is expected to be indeterminate.

Factors Influencing Supply of Rural Deposits

Studies on the supply of rural deposits can be subdivided into two types, descriptive and econometric. The descriptive category can be further subdivided into two types. The first argues (but does not necessarily provide empirical support to the intuitive conclusion) that the response of supply of financial savings to the (real) interest rate is positive but inelastic. These studies also suggest that savings would increase if the accessibility, safety, liquidity, and access to other financial and nonfinancial services were improved by the RFIs (Ahn, Adams, and Ro 1979; Akompong 1976; B. M. Desai 1983b; Kato 1966; Lee and Kim 1976; Ohio State University 1987; Paulson 1984; Penson 1972; Wiseman and Hitiris 1980). The second type of descriptive study, however, argues exactly the opposite, but also does not provide empirical support for these contentions. According to these studies, response of supply of rural deposits to the interest rate is not only positive but highly elastic.

They also suggest that raising deposit rates rather than improving density, accessibility, and other characteristics of RFIs should be accorded the highest priority in agricultural credit policy (Agabin 1987; Mooy 1974; Republic of Philippines 1979; and United Nations Secretariat 1980).

There are, however, seven econometric studies with 16 cases from which the relative importance of various price and nonprice factors that influence supply of rural deposits can be identified. These studies are on eight diverse countries—Bangladesh, India, Kenya, Nepal, Pakistan, Sri Lanka, Taiwan, and the United States. All of the studies except Penson (1972) use the single-equation ordinary least squares technique of estimation. Penson uses the two-stage least squares (2SLS) technique to take into account the simultaneity in the system of structural equations. Some of the independent variables in these studies are the same as those in the studies on rural loan demand: accessibility to RFIs, ability to save or borrow, and incentives to save or borrow. Results of these studies are reported in Tables 44-47.

The specified models explain a large proportion of variation in the supply of rural deposits. Most of the regression coefficients associated with the real interest rate have the expected positive sign, but only 8 out of 15 cases have a statistically significant coefficient. A large majority of coefficients related to noninterest rate factors have expected signs and are statistically significant.

These studies also show that the factors related to the noninterest rate are more important than the interest rate.[32] These factors, however, differ between LICs and MICs, on the one hand, and HICs, on the other, even though the percentage of variation explained by the models is the same across these countries. In LICs and MICs, these are, in order of importance, accessibility to deposit facilities and availability of nondeposit services such as loans and marketing services, ability to save, and interactions of these two. In HICs, the corresponding factors are rate of return (real) on competing forms of financial savings, expectations about availability of deposits, and the ability to save. The findings on LICs and MICs suggest that the future thrust of the institutional rural finance policy should be on improving accessibility of RFIs and on extending nondeposit services, both of which in turn would generate a greater ability to save. But the findings on HICs suggest that the thrust should be on improving the relative rate of return on deposits and on bettering the ability to save in financial forms, especially deposits.

Notwithstanding the importance of these results, none of the seven studies considers the response of financial savings to the rate of return on physical forms of savings. Similarly, these studies, with the exception of the two on the United States (Hamberger 1968; Penson 1972) do not examine the influence of the rate of return on competing forms of financial savings. Omission of these variables implies specification errors that are too serious to ignore, especially for understanding the saving

---

[32]For a similar finding on Third World countries, see Agabin 1987.

Table 44—Estimated multivariate models of supply of rural deposits in Kenya, 1970-82, and India, 1951-63

Determinant	Kenya, 1970-82 (Paulson 1984)			India, 1951-63 (Gupta 1970a)
	PCRSAV	PCFSAV	PCSD	PCRFS
Real interest rate[a]	0.43 (0.2)[4]	0.27 (0.1)[4]	1.88 (1.5)[3]	0.55 (2.9)*[2]
Number of bank branches	5.51 (3.6)*[1]	5.02 (3.3)*[1]	3.34 (5.1)*[1]	...
Per capita real GNP	0.20 (3.0)*[2]	0.20 (2.9)*[2]	0.05 (1.6)[2]	...
Per capita real permanent private income[b]	...	...	...	0.35 (17.2)*[1]
Per capita real permanent wealth[b]	...	...	...	0.01 (0.5)[3]
Time	−17.47 (−1.1)[3]	−16.93 (−1.1)[3]	1.22 (0.2)[4]	...
$\bar{R}^2$	0.98	0.99	0.99	0.75
Number of observations	13	13	13	11

Notes: Figures in parentheses are t-values. Figures in brackets are ranks based on magnitude of t-values (ignoring signs). Kenya is a middle-income African country and India is a low-income Asian country.

   PCRSAV = Per capita real savings and time deposits with commercial banks, nonbanking financial institutions, and post offices.

   PCFSAV = Per capita real savings and time deposits with commercial banks and nonbanking financial institutions.

   PCSD = PCRSAV plus deposits with savings and credit societies.

   PCRFS = Per capita real financing saving.

[a]The Kenyan study defines real interest rate as the nominal interest rate on savings deposits with commercial banks minus the inflation rate. The Indian study defines it as the nominal interest rate on savings deposits with post offices minus the inflation rate.
[b]Permanent private income is a three-year moving average.
*Significant at 1 percent.

behavior of the farm households in financial forms. The descriptive studies mentioned earlier become more interesting in this context.

They are also interesting because they convincingly show that there exists substantial capacity to save through deposits in the rural sector in such diverse LICs and MICs as Bangladesh, India, Indonesia, Malaysia, Republic of Korea, and Taiwan, where new technology in agriculture has been introduced. Another reason why some of these studies are useful is that they emphasize the importance of factors like easy access to financial saving facilities, liquidity, safety, and preferences of rural households for holding savings in the form of financial deposits (Kato

Table 45—Estimated multivariate models of supply of rural deposits in two studies of Asian low-income countries

Determinant	India, Nepal, Pakistan and Sri Lanka Together, 1970-81, PCRDSD (Srinivasan and Meyer 1986)		Bangladesh, India, Nepal, Pakistan, and Sri Lanka Together, 1970-81, PCRDSD (Srinivasan and Meyer 1986)	
	Model I	Model II	Model I	Model II
Real interest rate on 12-month time deposit	1.72 (3.1)*[6]	. . .	2.54 (5.4)*[7]	. . .
Nominal interest rate on 12-month time deposit	. . .	0.06 (0.6)[9]	. . .	0.13 (1.0)[11]
Inflation rate	. . .	−0.01 (−0.1)[10]	. . .	−0.68 (−1.7)**[8]
Number of bank branches per 1,000 inhabitants in rural areas	1.31 (18.8)*[1]	1.30 (19.3)*[1]	1.33 (15.6)*[1]	1.31 (12.4)*[1]
Per capita real agricultural GDP	0.53 (5.4)*[4]	0.62 (4.3)*[5]	0.59 (5.9)*[6]	0.72 (4.0)*[7]
Dummy variable for Sri Lanka	−4.24 (−8.8)*[3]	−4.21 (−9.0)*[3]	−4.32 (−9.6)*[2]	−4.10 (−7.6)*[2]
Dummy variable for Nepal	−0.96 (−1.2)[9]	−0.91 (−1.0)[8]	−1.32 (−1.8)**[11]	−1.07 (−1.2) [12]
Dummy variable for Pakistan	−3.38	−3.32	−3.57	−3.48
$\bar{R}^2$	0.88	0.87	0.98	0.97
Number of observations	12	12	12	12

Notes: Figures in parentheses are t-values. Figures in brackets are ranks based on magnitude of t-values (ignoring signs).

PCRDSD = Per capita real demand and savings deposits in rural areas.

*Significant at 1 percent.
**Significant at 5 percent.

1966; Lee and Kim 1976; Ohio State University 1987; Thingalaya 1980; Tuan 1973; van Wijnbergen 1983d; and Wiseman and Hitiris 1980).

The study on the Republic of Korea (Ahn, Adams, and Ro 1979) suggests that between 1961 and 1976 the farm households substituted liquid assets (such as cash, deposits, loaned money, and others) and physically productive resources for semiliquid assets (such as small animals, product inventories, and producer's material inventories). These substitutions may have been encouraged by higher returns on

Table 46—Relative importance of interest- and noninterest-rate-related determinants of supply of rural financial savings, Taiwan, 1960-70, and United States, 1948-70

Determinant	Taiwan, Provinces 1960-70 (Tuan 1973)			United States, Farm Sector 1948-70 (Penson 1972)	
	PFRDSD	PFRTD	PFRDSTD	RDDCB	RTSDCB
Real interest rate[a]	3*	5*	5*	4*	3*
Real agricultural output per farm-family	1*	3*	2*	...	...
Value of loan business, per member of farmers associations	2	1*	1*	...	
Expenses on extension services per member of farmers associations	4	4*	3*	...	...
Incomes from marketing of farm produce, farm inputs, and consumer goods per member of farmers associations	5	2*	4*		
Real rate of return on marketable bonds	...	...	...	2*	1*
Real rate of return on equities	...	...	...	3*	
Real gross farm plus nonfarm personal income	...	...	...	...	6**
Real value of stock of physical assets	...	...	...	6	5**
Service charge rate on demand deposits	...	...	...	1*	4*
Lagged dependent variable	...	...	...	5	2*
R^2	0.98	0.99	0.99	...	...
Number of observations	11	11	11	23	23

Notes: PFRDSD = Per farm-family real demand and saving deposits;
PFRTD = Per farm-family real time deposits;
PFRDSTD = PFRDSD + PFRTD;
RDDCB = Real demand deposits with commercial banks;
RTSDCB = Real time and savings deposits with commercial banks.

[a]In the Taiwanese study, real interest rate is the simple average of the nominal interest rate on demand and savings deposits, that on time deposits, and that on all three types of deposits minus the inflation rate.
*Significant at 1 percent.
**Significant at 5 percent.

savings in the form of physical productive farm resources induced by technological change. Better and more accessible nonfinancial services extended by the agricultural cooperatives may also have played a part.

There are two reasons why these noninterest-rate-related factors may have influenced substitutability more than the interest rate. First,

Table 47—Relative importance of interest- and noninterest-rate-related determinants of supply of rural financial savings in a study of the United States

Determinant	United States, All Households, Semiannual Observations, 1952-62 (Hamberger 1968)		
	TSDCB	SDOFI	CWLIC
Real interest rate on savings and time deposits	2*	4*	3*
Real interest rate on savings with other financial institutions	5	3*	...
Real interest rate on marketable bonds	4***	5*	...
Real aggregate household income	...	...	4
Real value of financial net worth	3*	2*	...
Real value of financial assets	...	...	2
Lagged dependent variable	1	1	1
R^2	0.99	0.99	0.99
Number of observations	22	22	22

Notes: For this U.S. study, the real interest rate is the nominal interest rate on time deposits minus inflation rate.

  TSDCB = Time and savings deposits with commercial banks in real terms;
  SDOFI = Savings deposits with other financial institutions in real terms;
  CWLIC = Claims with insurance companies in real terms.

  *Significant at 1 percent.
***Significant at 10 percent.

the share of cash, in addition to deposits, in total assets held by the farmers increased during the period. Second, a simple exercise of regressing real deposits collected by the agricultural cooperatives on the real interest rate on deposits (given in Lee, Kim, and Adams 1977) shows that deposits do not respond to changes in the interest rate. This inelastic response of deposits to the interest rate is also found for all forms of financial savings collected by the agricultural cooperatives in the Republic of Korea.

Many descriptive studies rightly recognize that decisions of farm households to produce, consume, and save or invest are tightly intertwined. They also emphasize the role that incentives to save play in promoting savings, especially in financial forms. Two types of incentives are stressed in Adams 1978; Adams, Ahn, and Hyun 1977; Ahn, Adams, and Ro 1979; Lee, Kim, and Adams 1977; and Mauri 1977. One of these is the rate of return on farm investment and the other is the rate of return on financial deposits. These studies contend that it is hard to sort out the influence on savings of an increase in the real rate of interest paid on savings deposits, though it is likely that overall savings would increase as a result of an increase in the real interest rate. This is not correct. On the contrary, when the rate of interest on deposits increases, the amount of deposits supplied by the rural sector should increase, but the resulting change in the overall amount of savings is indeterminate a priori.

The positive response of supply of deposits to the interest rate follows directly from standard economics and from the theory of portfolio balance. The impact of the rise in the real interest rate on overall savings (physical plus financial) cannot be determined because of the ambiguous nature of its income effect, although the substitution effect is positive (see B. M. Desai 1983b; Miksell and Zinser 1973; and Snyder 1974).

Response of Rural Deposits to the Interest Rate

As mentioned earlier, some descriptive studies (Adams 1978; Ahn, Adams, and Ro 1979; Lee and Kim 1976; Mooy 1974) contend that the response of rural deposits to the interest rate is highly elastic, though they do not provide the empirical value of this elasticity (Table 48). Other descriptive studies argue that this response is interest-inelastic (see, for example, Akompong 1976). However, six out of the eight econometric studies presented in Table 48 show that when the real interest rate increases by 1 percentage point, the supply of rural deposits increases by much less than 1 percent. This is the case for countries as diverse as the United States, India, Kenya, the Republic of Korea, and Taiwan.[33] Six studies (Paulson 1984; Gupta 1970a; Lee and Kim 1976; Tuan 1973; Hamberger 1968; and Penson 1972) on these five countries show that the interest elasticity of deposits is lowest in MICs (0.002-0.02), followed by LICs (0.16), and then HICs (0.33-0.87). It is noteworthy that this estimate for LICs, unlike those for MICs and HICs,[34] is for all households, both farm and nonfarm. Hence, judging the potential of interest rate policy to induce farm households to save in the form of financial deposits should be undertaken with great caution. This holds even for the two econometric studies by Srinivasan and Meyer (1986; n.d.) showing that the response of rural deposits mobilized by the commercial banks to the interest rate is highly elastic in four or five South Asian countries taken together (India, Nepal, Pakistan, Sri Lanka, and additionally Bangladesh) (Table 48).

The two South Asian studies have some other severe limitations. First, they consider the interest rate on 12-month time deposits, even though the dependent variable is savings, time, and demand deposits. Second, they do not estimate the response of financial deposits to the interest rate for each individual country. Instead, they pull together data for four or five countries in which the commercial banking and economic (including the tertiary or service sector) structure in rural areas is very diverse and at different levels of development. Third, neither of

---

[33]The Republic of Korea and Taiwan are often cited as successful examples of the strong inducement provided to the supply of deposits by high interest rates on deposits, but this contention does not hold when examined empirically.

[34]Even for HICs, the elasticity estimate for farm households is much lower than that for all households, the former being 0.33-0.42, while the latter is 0.66-0.87. Nonetheless, the interest elasticity of farm deposits in HICs is more than twice the value for LICs.

Table 48—Evidence on elasticity of supply of rural financial savings to the real interest rate in selected developing and developed countries

Region/Country	Perfectly Elastic	Highly Elastic	Moderately Elastic	Not Inelastic	Perfectly Inelastic
Sub-Saharan Africa					
Middle-income countries					
Ghana (Akompong 1976)	...	...	...	...	a
Kenya (Paulson 1984)	...	...	...	...	Close to zero[b]
Asia					
Low-income countries					
India (Adams 1978)	...	a	...	...	...
India, all households (Gupta 1970a)	...	...	...	0.16[b]	...
Indonesia (Mooy 1974)	...	a	...	...	...
Four South Asian countries together (Srinivasan and Meyer 1986)	1.72[c]	...	...	...	...
Five South Asian countries together (Srinvasan and Meyer 1986)	2.54[d]	...	...	...	...
Middle-income countries					
Malaysia (Adams 1978)	...	a	...	...	...
Korea, Republic of (Lee and Kim 1976)	...	a	...	...	...
Korea, Republic of (Adams 1978)	...	a	...	...	...
Korea, Republic of (Ahn, Adams, and Ro 1979)	...	a	...	...	...
Taiwan (Adams 1978)	...	a	...	...	-0.02-0.01[e]
Taiwan (Tuan 1973)	...	...	...	...	0.002-0.02[f]
High-income countries					
Japan (Adams 1978)	...	a	...	...	...
North America					
High-income country					
United States, all households (Hamberger 1968)	...	0.66-0.87[g]	...	...	...
United States, farm sector (Penson 1972)	...	...	0.33-0.42[h]	...	...

[a]Discusses the interest rate response, but does not give any empirical estimation.
[b]Based on a multivariate single-equation linear model. The Kenyan model uses institutional data on rural deposits. The Indian model is for all households. Interest elasticity was estimated by the authors by utilizing this model and data on the interest rate, inflation rate, and financial savings.
[c]Based on a multivariate pooled time-series *cum* cross-section single equation model utilizing data for 1970-81 for India, Nepal, Pakistan, and Sri Lanka. The dependent variable is demand plus savings deposits collected by the commercial banks from rural areas. A double-log form of function is estimated.
[d]Based on a multivariate pooled time-series *cum* cross-section single equation model utilizing data for 1970-81 for India, Nepal, Pakistan, and Sri Lanka; and 1972-83 for Bangladesh. The dependent variable is demand plus savings deposits collected by the commercial banks from rural areas. A double-log form of function is estimated.

(continued)

Table 48—Continued

[e]Based on the authors' estimation of the single-equation univariate linear model, using the institutional data on rural bank deposits given in Lee and Kim 1976.

[f]Based on multivariate single-equation linear models. The study uses time-series data from 292 farmers' associations at the provincial level. The dependent variables are demand deposits, term deposits, and both of these together.

[g]Based on multivariate single-equation linear models for all households. The study uses semi-annual observations for 1952-62. Dependent variables are time and savings deposits at commercial banks, savings deposits with other financial institutions, and claims on insurance companies.

[h]Based on a multivariate, reduced form of linear model for the farm sector. The study uses time-series data for 1948-70. The dependent variables are demand deposits and time and savings deposits of the farm sector.

these studies considers the effects of the real rate of return on other forms of financial savings, or on physical forms of savings, the importance of which may differ greatly in the countries covered. And fourth, these studies do not define what is rural. Thus, it is clear from the remaining six econometric studies that raising the interest rate on deposits by 1 percentage point increases farm deposits only modestly in HICs and hardly at all in MICs and LICs.

From the preceding discussion, it may be concluded that a policy of raising interest rates on farmers' deposits cannot be the kingpin for mobilizing these deposits during the development process. Future policy for developing countries should concentrate on improving accessibility, liquidity, safety, and nondeposit services such as credit, input sales, and the character of deposit facilities of the RFIs. In operational terms, this implies increasing the number of field-level rural offices; making it possible to deposit for a shorter period of time, from a few weeks up to six months, with commensurate interest rates; protecting deposit facilities from theft and misuse; and improving credit and input-linked deposit instruments.

8

Response of Supply of Rural Saving to Interest Rate and Nonprice Determinants

Thisis chapter discusses factors influencing the supply of rural saving. It also analyzes whether the impact of the real rate of return on saving is positive and elastic and why. Finally, implications for rural institutional finance policy are drawn.

Factors Influencing Rural Saving

Rural, or for that matter economy-wide, saving includes both physical productive resources and financial forms. This is so in any country. In an early stage of development, physical productive saving dominates total saving, especially where agriculture is not commercialized and new technology has not been adopted. Even when these constraints are relaxed, farmers' preference for physical productive saving remains high. This is because they acquire new forms of real resources associated with technological change that act as an altogether different source of capital formation and hence income. Farmers' higher preference to hold savings or assets in physical productive resources is found in Bangladesh, India, the Philippines, Thailand, the Republic of Korea, Taiwan, and Japan. Data for the Philippines and Japan are given in Table 49.

Having seen the nature of the dependent variable—rural or economy-wide saving—the question arises as to how it is defined in the literature under review. Gupta 1970b, one of four studies on rural saving, defines it as a residual of income minus consumption. The other three (B.M. Desai 1975; Ong 1972; and Hyun, Adams, and Hushak 1979) define it as consumption, which is the other side of the same coin in this method. This is also the case with a study of the United States (Boskin 1978), which deals with private-sector saving. Another study on the Republic of Korea (Yusuf and Peters 1984) uses economy-wide saving—either domestic or national—derived by the residual method of measuring saving. The remaining four studies (Williamson 1968; Friend 1963; Giovannini 1983; and, again, Williamson 1968) use the same method, but for personal economy-wide saving, which largely occurs in the household sector.

The literature considers price and nonprice factors as determinants of saving. In this context, price factors are represented by some measure of expected real rate of return and may be termed "incentive to save." Conceptually, this should be a weighted average of rates of return on

Table 49—Pattern of total rural savings and assets in the Philippines and Japan

Type of Savings	The Philippines (Subido 1961)			Japan (Higuchi and Kawamura 1988)			
	Increase (Decrease) in Average Household Saving	Percentage of Total		1965		1984	
		Assets	Saving				
	(pesos)	(percent)		(Y1,000)	(percent)	(Y1,000)	(percent)
Physical savings	882	109.0	172.6	1,961.4	72.1	15,811.5	54.0
Land acquisition	95	11.7	18.5	...	...	...	...
Land infrastructure	19	2.3	3.7	...	...	...	...
Machinery and implements	159	19.7	31.1	...	...	...	...
Building and structure	140	17.3	27.4	...	...	...	...
Livestock and poultry	233	28.8	45.6	...	...	...	...
Inventory	119	14.7	23.3	91.0	3.3	164.1	0.6
Major consumer durables	117	14.5	23.0	...	...	...	...
Financial savings	(−73)	(−9.0)	(−14.3)	757.6	27.9	13,446.8	46.0
Gross asset acquisition	809	100.0	158.3	2,719.0	100.0	29,258.3	100.0
Increase (decrease) in liabilities	298	36.8	(−58.3)	...	...	...	...
Total saving	511	63.2	100.0	...	...	...	...

Note: Figures in parentheses indicate a decrease.

different forms of saving minus the expected rate of inflation, which entails many complex conceptual, methodological, and time-consuming data problems that are difficult to resolve. Most studies, therefore, use the nominal interest rate on one or the other form of financial saving minus the expected inflation rate. This implies a perfectly competitive capital market, which equalizes the marginal rate of return on each of the different forms of saving. But "capital market" is imperfect by definition because it deals in future transactions. Moreover, in the agricultural production process, many forms of capital are complementary, and some even augment labor use, making it difficult to measure marginal rates of return to capital or saving. And finally, care must be taken in deriving policy implications from the impact of the real interest rate on saving, which is not always the case in the literature reviewed.

Three of the four studies on rural saving measure incentive to save as gross farm revenue divided by working capital investment, or by the value of farm assets other than land, or by operating farm assets lagged one year (B. M. Desai 1975; Hyun, Adams, and Hushak 1979; Ong 1972). The fourth (Gupta 1970b) measures it as interest rate on treasury bills minus the expected inflation rate. A study of the United States measures incentives to save as net revenue from all properties divided by the value of all assets minus the expected inflation rate (Boskin 1978). All of the remaining five studies (Friend 1963; Giovannini 1983; Houthakker 1965; Williamson 1968; Yusuf and Peters 1984) consider the nominal rate of interest on 12-month deposits minus the expected inflation rate. Most studies measure the expected rate of inflation as a weighted average of the past three or five years' actual inflation rate.

Nonprice factors in the 10 studies include such determinants as permanent and transitory income, wealth, family size, dependency ratio in the family, farm size, source of income, liquid assets, foreign saving, and inflation rate. These essentially represent the ability to save.

Seven of the 10 studies estimate a single-equation saving function by utilizing an ordinary least squares (OLS) statistical procedure, while the remaining three are based on a two-stage, least-squares instrumental variables (2SLSIV) technique (Boskin 1978; Friend 1963; Giovannini 1983). This is perhaps because it is difficult to specify, estimate, and understand the results of a simultaneous system. Despite the lack of uniformity in the definitions of saving and its determinants, as well as the estimation methods, it is instructive to consider these studies together and those that address the issue of saving in descriptive terms.

The four studies on rural saving that quantitatively allow for analysis of both the ability to save and incentives are those on India (B. M. Desai 1975; Gupta 1970b), the Republic of Korea (Hyun, Adams, and Hushak 1979), and Taiwan (Ong 1972). The six studies (Gupta 1970c; Yusuf and Peters 1984; Friend 1963; Boskin 1978; Williamson 1968; and Giovannini 1983) that analyze economy-wide savings are those on Burma (Myanmar), India, Malaysia, the Philippines, Singapore, the Republic of Korea, Taiwan, Japan, and the United States. But there are as many as 21 other studies that examine the ability to save quantitatively and incentives to save in qualitative terms. Another group of 22 studies deals descriptively with either ability or incentive to save or both. All these studies show that there is substantial saving even in developing countries and, more important, in their rural sectors. The rest of the chapter deals largely with the 10 quantitative studies, with occasional reference to the other studies.

The results of 18 cases from the 10 quantitative studies are reported in Tables 50-53. With only a few exceptions, the specified models explain a large proportion of the variation in rural saving. A number of regression coefficients associated with the various explanatory variables are statistically significant. These tables also show the relative importance of price and nonprice factors in influencing rural and economy-wide saving. In Asia, nonprice factors are more important than price factors, no

Table 50—Estimated multivariate models of supply of rural saving in two studies of India

| Variable | India (Gupta 1970b) | | | A District in India (B. M. Desai 1975) |
	Personal Saving per Capita	Urban Household Saving	Rural Household Saving	Rural Household Consumption
Permanent income	0.17 (0.6)[3]	0.42 (3.3)*[1]	0.02 (8.6)*[2]	...
Transitory income	−0.48 (−2.6)*[1]	−0.32 (−1.5)[3]	0.04 (9.3)*[1]	...
Disposable private income (current/lagged)	...	...	...	0.50 (3.6)*[2]
Inverse of disposable private income of the previous year	...	...	...	−6,047.39 (−0.4)[5]
Value of farm plus non-farm assets (excluding land)	...	...	...	0.94 (0.09)[4]
Family size	...	...	...	34.45 (4.7)*[1]
Interaction of rate of return to working capital and disposable private income	...	...	...	−0.14 (−2.6)*[3]
Real rate of interest	5.01 (2.5)*[2]	5.06 (2.5)*[2]	0.007 (1.0)[3]	...
$\bar{R}^2$	0.68	0.67	0.94	0.52
Number of observations	17	13	13	85

Note: Figures in parentheses are t-values, and figures in brackets are rank based on magnitude of the t-value (ignoring signs).
*Significant at 1 percent.

Table 51—Estimated multivariate models of supply of rural saving in selected studies of Asian countries

| Variable | Asian Middle-Income Countries (Williamson 1968) | | | | | Taiwan (Ong 1972) |
	Burma PSPC	India PSPC	Philippines PSPC	Republic of Korea PSPC	Taiwan PSPC	Rural Household Consumption per Capita
Permanent income	0.10 (1.0)[2]	-0.16 (-0.3)[1]	-0.26 (-3.2)*[1]	-0.07 (-0.5)[2]	0.30 (3.1)*[1]	...
Transitory income	1.04 (1.0)***[1]	0.08 (0.18)[2]	0.85 (2.0)**[2]	1.09 (1.2)[1]	-0.15 (-0.3)[3]	...
Lagged dependent variable	...	...	...	...	...	0.33 (7.1)*[2]
Rate of return to all assets in previous year	...	...	...	...	...	-1.58 (-1.7)[3]
Real rate of interest	0.02 (0.2)[3]	-0.04 (-0.17)[3]	-0.30 (-1.6)***[3]	-0.002 (-0.1)[3]	-0.07 (-0.8)[2]	...
Real per capita income	...	...	...	...	...	0.38 (18.8)*[1]
Ratio of farm income to family income	...	...	...	...	...	5.93 (1.5)***[4]
R^2	0.37	0.13	0.75	0.34	0.67	0.70
Number of observations	12	8	13	8	12	n.a.

Notes: PSPC is personal saving per capita. Figures in parentheses are t-values, and the figures in brackets are rank based on magnitude of the t-value (ignoring signs). n.a. is not available.
*Significant at 1 percent.
**Significant at 5 percent.
***Significant at 10 percent.

Table 52—Estimated multivariate models of supply of rural saving in the Republic of Korea

| Variable | Republic of Korea (Hyun, Adams, and Hushak 1979) | | Republic of Korea (Yusuf and Peters 1984) | |
	Rural Household Consumption per Capita	Rural Household Consumption	Gross National Savings	Gross Domestic Savings
Permanent income	0.96 (8.3)*[1]	1.11 (5.7)*[1]	. . .	. . .
Transitory income	0.23 (0.1)[7]	−0.01 (−0.1)[7]	. . .	. . .
Growth rate in real GNP/GDP	. . .	. . .	1.00 (3.4)*[2]	1.71 (6.9)*[2]
Inflation rate	. . .	. . .	1.07 (2.3)*[4]	1.42 (3.8)*[3]
Real rate of interest	. . .	. . .	1.16 (2.9)*[30]	0.50 (50.6)*[1]
Level of real GNP/GDP	. . .	. . .	1.56 (24.1)*[1]	1.87 (50.6)*[1]
Interaction of permanent income with cultivated land	−0.20 (−1.20)[4]	−0.17 (−0.6)[6]	. . .	. . .
Interaction of permanent income with rate of return to capital	0.02 (0.6)[5]	0.051 (1.5)[2]	. . .	. . .
Interaction of permanent income with source of income	−0.34 (−0.3)[6]	−0.36 (−1.1)[4]	. . .	. . .
Interaction of permanent income with value of liquid assets	−0.0007 (−1.3)[3]	−0.0005 (−1.3)[3]	. . .	. . .
Interaction of permanent income with dependency ratio in the family	−0.05 (−1.4)[2]	0.13 (1.0)[5]	. . .	. . .
$\bar{R}^2$	0.92	0.93	0.98	0.99
Number of observations	131	131	18	18

Notes: Figures in parentheses are t-values, and the figures in brackets are rank based on magnitude of the t-value (ignoring signs).
*Significant at 1 percent.

matter what the income level of the country. The same is true for the United States.

Among the four studies on rural saving, B. M. Desai's 1975 study of an Indian district reveals that family size is the most important determinant, followed by lagged current income, then interaction of the expected rate of return and income, wealth (a proxy for initial endow-

Table 53—Estimated multivariate models of supply of rural saving in selected developing and developed countries

Variable	Seven Asian Countries[a] Ratio of Domestic Savings to Gross National Product		Japan Personal Saving per Capita (Williamson 1968)	United States Private Consumption per Capita (Boskin 1978)
	Friend 1963	Giovannini 1983		
Permanent income	...	...	0.30 (16.1)*[1]	...
Transitory income	...	...	0.64 (2.6)*[3]	...
Disposable private income	...	...	...	0.55 (4.2)*[2]
Lagged value of disposable private income	...	...	...	0.32 (1.4)[6]
Lagged market value of private nonhuman wealth	...	...	...	0.72 (24.0)*[1]
Growth rate in real GNP/GDP	0.21 (1.9)**[4]	0.40 (1.8)**[2]	...	...
Lagged dependent variable	0.15 (1.4)[5]	0.78 (4.5)*[1]	...	...
Foreign savings/GNP	-0.46 (-3.8)*[2]	0.04 (0.3)[5]	...	...
Unemployment rate	...	...	...	-0.03 (-2.2)*[4]
Expected inflation rate	...	...	...	-0.36 (-1.7)**[5]
Real interest rate/real rate of return to capital	0.15 (2.1)**[3]	-0.01 (-0.7)[4]	-0.76 (-3.0)*[2]	-2.28 (-3.7)*[3]
Level of real per capita income	0.13 (5.8)*[1]	0.04 (0.8)[3]	...	...
$\bar{R}^2$	0.84	0.91	0.97	0.99
Number of observations	70	101	13	35

Notes: Figures in parentheses are t-values, and the figures in brackets are rank based on magnitude of the t-value (ignoring signs).
[a]Countries covered are Burma (now Myanmar), India, Republic of Korea, Malaysia, the Philippines, Singapore, and Taiwan. Pooled time series from 1962 to 1972 are utilized in Friend 1963, and those from 1962 to 1980 are utilized in Giovannini 1983.
*Significant at 1 percent.
**Significant at 5 percent.

ment), and lastly, the inverse of lagged current income (Table 50). This study also shows that the marginal propensity to save with respect to expected family income increases by 33 percent when the expected rate of return is included.

In Ong's 1972 study of Taiwan, the expected rate of return variable, among others, is included, and expected income is the most important variable (Table 51). In the Republic of Korea (Hyun, Adams, and Hushak 1979), permanent income is the most important variable, while transitory income is the least important (Table 52). Even this study shows that the marginal propensity to save is sensitive to the exclusion of the expected rate of return to capital as an explanatory variable. Among other variables that are more important than incentives to save are interaction of permanent income with (1) the dependency ratio in the family, (2) the value of liquid assets, and (3) cultivated land. But, when rural saving is defined per household instead of per capita, then interaction of permanent income with the rate of return to capital is the second most important factor. In Gupta's (1970b) study on rural household saving in India, transitory income is the most important variable, followed by permanent income, and then the real rate of interest on treasury bills (Table 50). Among the remaining six studies on economy-wide saving, the majority show that incentive to save is the least important variable. This is also the case with gross national saving in the Republic of Korea. In the United States, incentives to save are broadly more significant than some of the measures of ability to save, though the latter, with its more direct measurement, is more important than the real rate of return to capital (Boskin 1978) (Table 53). In conclusion, in all the countries under reference, ability to save is more important than incentives to save.

Response of Rural Saving to the Interest Rate

As mentioned earlier in the context of total saving, the interest rate on deposits is a proxy for the rate of return to capital because of the difficulty of measuring the true determinant. Despite this difficulty, this determinant has been studied in three papers on rural saving (B.M. Desai 1975; Hyun, Adams, and Hushak 1979; and Ong 1972) and one on economy-wide private-sector saving (Boskin 1978). Irrespective of the nature of the measurement of the variable on incentive to save, it is not possible to guess whether its impact on saving will be positive or negative (B. M. Desai 1983b; Miksell and Zinser 1973; Snyder 1974). Nor can the magnitude of its elasticity be hypothesized because, when the variable for incentive to save improves, two types of effects result: one is a pure substitution effect and the other is an income effect. The substitution effect is always positive because savers will substitute future consumption for present consumption, and consequently they will save more when the expected rate of return increases. The income effect is indeterminate, as shown in B. M. Desai 1983b. It can be negative or positive.

When the present value of net income increases after a rise in the interest rate or the rate of return, savers will decrease saving and increase consumption. If, on the contrary, the value of net income decreases, then they will increase saving and reduce current consumption. The former scenario may occur when there is a surplus in an earlier period, but a deficit in a later period. In this case, the impact on income would be negative; hence, the positive substitution effect can be fully or partially offset. Whether the total impact is positive, negative, or zero in this scenario cannot be predicted, and it is an empirical question. The scenario of decrease in net income can occur when there is a deficit in an earlier period and a surplus in a later period, leading to a positive effect on income that reinforces the (pure) positive substitution effect of the rise in the real rate of return. Here, the total impact is positive.[35]

Empirical evidence shows that the total impact on rural saving of improving the incentive to save is positive. Among the five studies on rural saving (Gupta 1970b; B.M. Desai 1975; Hyun, Adams, and Hushak 1979; Ong 1972; and, again, Hyun, Adams, and Hushak 1979), four studies with two cases on India and one each on the Republic of Korea and Taiwan reveal that when the rate of return improves, saving increases and current consumption declines. But the study on the Republic of Korea, which specifies saving per capita instead of per household, shows exactly the opposite (Table 54). This suggests that this study should have captured the effect of family size separately to validate more clearly the impact of the rate of return on rural saving, holding other factors constant. Moreover, among the remaining 13 cases, as many as 6 also show the response to the rate of return to be positive. Most of these cases are on the same countries. But, a study that includes both Asian LICs and MICs shows this response to be positive for 1962-72 (Friend 1963), and another on these same countries shows it to be negative for 1962-80 (Giovannini 1985). The strength of these highly aggregative studies is, however, doubtful.

Evidence showing that incentives to save have a positive impact on rural saving are the result of very high positive substitution effects, which may have more than offset any possible negative income impact or been reinforced by a positive income effect. These may have been induced by rapid and widespread technological change in agriculture in these countries or in the sample areas. This may hold even for the positive impact of the interest rate on gross domestic saving in the Republic of Korea. It may also be the case for private economy-wide saving in the United States (Boskin 1978), where technological change has occurred in all sectors. All these studies show that the response of saving to the real rate of return is not elastic, elasticity being 0.00005 to 0.50 at the most (Table 54).[36]

---

[35]Despite these complexities, some studies contend that when the interest rate increases, saving invariably increases and is elastic to this rate (see, for example, Adams 1978). What these studies probably consider "saving" is saving in financial deposits alone, which is obviously positively related to the interest rate. But, even this saving is not interest-rate-elastic as discussed in Chapter 7 (Sahani 1967; United Nations Secretariat 1980; Vardachary 1980; Wiseman and Hitiris 1980).

[36]Iqbal (1982) estimates that this elasticity is less than 0.25 for a large sample of rural households (2,739 in number) in India. It also shows that the ability to save influences rural saving more than the interest rate. This study is not reviewed in greater detail because it estimates this elasticity for nominal interest rates.

Table 54—Positive and negative effects of the rate of return on total saving in selected studies of various countries

Country	Study	Data Presented	Period
Positive			
India	Gupta 1970b	Urban household real saving	1950-62
India	Gupta 1970b	Rural household real saving	1950-62
India, Surat District	B. M. Desai 1975	Rural household consumption	1970-71
India	Gupta 1970c	Personal saving per capita	1950-66
Korea, Republic of	Hyun, Adams, and Hushak 1979	Farm household consumption	1970
Korea, Republic of	Yusuf and Peters 1984	Gross national real saving, elasticity is 1.16	1965-82
Korea, Republic of	Yusuf and Peters 1984	Gross domestic real saving, elasticity is 0.50	1965-82
Seven Asian countries combined[a]	Friend 1963	Ratio of domestic real saving to gross national product	1962-72
Taiwan	Ong 1972	Farm household consumption per capita, cross-section cum time series pooled data, elasticity ranges from −0.00005 to −0.00035	1960-70
United States	Boskin 1978	Private real consumption per capita, elasticity is −0.40	1929-49
Negative			
Burma	Williamson 1968	Personal real saving per capita	1950-64
India	Williamson 1968	Personal real saving per capita	1950-64
Japan	Williamson 1968	Personal real saving per capita	1950-64
Korea, Republic of	Williamson 1968	Personal real saving per capita	1950-64
Korea, Republic of	Hyun, Adams, and Hushak 1979	Farm household consumption per capita	1970
Philippines	Williamson 1968	Personal real saving per capita	1950-64
Seven Asian countries combined[a]	Giovannini 1983	Ratio of domestic real saving to gross national product	1962-80
Taiwan	Williamson 1968	Personal real saving per capita	1950-64

[a]Countries covered are Burma (now Myanmar), India, Republic of Korea, Malaysia, the Philippines, Singapore, and Taiwan.

In order for rural saving to respond positively to incentives to save, what is needed is rapid and widespread technological change, which accelerates the ability to save and the rates of return. The higher rates of return associated with technological change would make saving more attractive and thereby would enlarge the positive substitution effect, offsetting any growth in its negative income impact. In addition to encouraging income growth in the agricultural sector, this would result in higher capital formation, which in turn would increase the need for financial services. Through this mechanism, scale and scope economies for the viability of rural financial institutions would also improve. To accomplish this, agricultural credit policy should aim at improving vertical organization, density, coverage of farmers, and the number of functions performed by RFIs, besides maintaining interest rates that are conducive to investment.

9

Flow of Funds of the Rural Financial Institutional System

The issue of how growth and development of a rural financial institutional (RFI) system affects the flow of public resources is important. Increasing public resources through the tax system has a negative effect on incentives, which increases disproportionately as the level of taxation rises. At the same time, the requirements for investment in public goods are immense. This is particularly the case for rural development, where the private operating units tend to be small, hence requiring public provision of many services that large firms can provide in the private sector. Although the total resources that can be raised from rural saving are immense because of the extent of the RFI system, opportunities for leakage through subsidies, poor administration, and corruption are also great.

A widespread belief that an RFI system is generally inefficient, undisciplined, and often corrupt has led to a negative attitude about such institutions, and an implicit view that they represent a huge net drain on public revenues, for which the return is of doubtful value. However, this view arises from a gross oversimplification of the flow of funds associated with an RFI system.

In tackling this issue, this chapter first outlines a framework to examine whether an RFI system is a net drain on or a contributor to public resources. This framework is general in nature to account for both the unifunctional and multifunctional roles of this system in agricultural development. The chapter also discusses some determinants of the net contribution of a system. Finally, a comparison is made between an improvement in the functions of an RFI system and an increase in interest rates to determine which option has the largest impact on net contribution, profit, and unit transaction costs of the system. This analysis is based on stylized data that are partially derived from earlier chapters, since actual data are not available.

Framework for Determining the Net Flow of Funds of an RFI System

Visualize an RFI system that has the following inflows during any given year:
- Equity capital
- Reserves
- Deposits

115

- Other borrowings
- Purchase of farm inputs, consumer goods, and so forth
- Loans recovered (principal)
- Interest revenue from loans recovered
- Noninterest revenue from nonfund-based activities, such as bank guarantees, check-clearing fees, and discounts on bills, and from sale of farm inputs, consumer goods, and so forth
- Subsidies for administrative costs

Let the sum of these nine variables be termed inflows to this system.

Similarly, an RFI system has the following outflows during the same year:

- Loans made or issued, including rescheduled loans
- Investments made in deposits, securities, and so forth
- Share capital withdrawn or matured (excluding dividends paid)
- Deposits withdrawn (excluding interest paid)
- Other borrowings repaid (principal only)
- Sale of farm inputs, produce, and so forth
- Bad and doubtful debts
- Interest paid on deposits
- Interest paid on other borrowings
- Transaction costs

Let the sum of these 10 variables be termed outflows of the system.

The difference between the sum of inflows and that of outflows is termed net inflows (+)/outflows (−). This difference can either be positive, negative, or zero. When it is positive, it implies that the RFI system under consideration is a net contributor to public resources. If it is negative, it suggests that this system is a net drain on public resources. If it is zero, it obviously means that the system is neither a drain nor a contributor to public resources.

Application of this framework to time-series data requires that each variable be measured in real terms. For this, the agricultural GDP deflator is an obvious deflator.

Determinants of Net Inflow/Outflow of an RFI System

Having stated how to determine whether an RFI system is a drain on or a contributor to public resources, it is necessary to understand why net inflow/outflow occurs and how and why it changes over time or differs across countries.

A priori determinants that might answer these questions cannot be specified because each system differs in its assets, liabilities, and the structure of its related financial and nonfinancial services. Broadly, however, these factors would be related to either interest or nonprice factors. Some of these have been discussed in previous chapters, including deposits and loans (for example, interest rates, access to RFIs, and safety and liquidity of deposit facilities), interest and noninterest revenue, interest and noninterest costs, and time profile of maturity of interest revenue and payment. Depending on their relevance to a given RFI system, these determinants could be used in evaluating the contribution of the RFI system.

Regarding factors influencing loan recoveries, review of available literature suggests that they are largely in the realm of the noninterest-rate variables that characterize the operations of an RFI as unifunctional or multifunctional (Appendix 2).

One conclusion is obvious: the positive or negative contribution of an RFI system is influenced by many complex and interacting factors rather than a single factor such as rural deposits mobilized, loans recovered, or costs controlled. And measures to raise or lower one element may have an obverse effect on others. For example, closing an RFI that has a poor loan recovery rate may lose a large amount of potential incremental deposits; raising interest rates may reduce sales of inputs, thus slowing production increases and reducing the next round of deposits; or alternatively, it may provide funds to open more branches and bring in more deposits.

Improving the Functions of an RFI System Compared with Increasing Interest Rates: Effects on Net Contribution, Profit, and Unit Transaction Costs

In the earlier chapters, it was shown that improving the functions of an RFI system is more likely to achieve basic policy goals than an upward revision in interest rates. This, however, should not be interpreted to mean that interest rates should never be raised. What it implies is that promotion of vertical and horizontal integration of the functions of an RFI system is critical. Similarly, it is necessary to maintain interest rates that are conducive to the three basic objectives of agricultural credit policy, namely, rural growth with equity, rural financial market integration, and scale economies in costs to improve the viability of RFIs.

In this section, an attempt is made to show that improving the functional structure of an RFI system enables it to make a larger net contribution to public resources, to increase its profitability, and to make more effective and efficient use of its transaction costs than would result from raising interest rates. To demonstrate this comparatively static impact, three scenarios are conceptualized: the base scenario in which an RFI system is unifunctional and a level of interest rates is set (scenario I); a second scenario in which the RFI system is multifunctional, and interest rates are at the same level as in the base scenario (scenario II); and a third scenario in which interest rates are raised by 200 percent but the functional structure of the RFI system is unifunctional, as in the base scenario (scenario III).

Empirical validation of these scenarios requires data on those variables listed under the framework for determining net contribution, profits, and unit transaction costs. These data are not available in the literature under study. However, data on some parameters such as loan delinquency rates and interest rate elasticities of both rural loan demand and rural deposit supply are available. On the basis of these data and hypothetical values of the other variables and the analysis in the preceding chapters, Table 55 is prepared.

Table 55—Impact of horizontally and vertically integrating a rural financial institution system compared with increasing interest rates on net contribution, profits, and unit transaction costs of this system

Inflow and Outflow Items	Scenario I[a]	Scenario II[b]	Scenario III[c]
	(US$ million)		
Inflows			
1. Equity capital	60	100	60
2. Reserves	20	20	20
3. Deposits	0	100[d]	32[e]
4. Other borrowings	200	300	0[f]
5. Value of nonfinancial activities of inputs, consumer goods, farm produce, and so forth	0	180	0
6. Loan recovery (principal)	110[g]	394[h]	27[i]
7. Interest revenue on inflow item 6 and outflow item 2	17[j]	50[k]	27[l]
8. Noninterest revenue	0	20[m]	0
9. Administrative cost subsidy	0	0	0
10. Sum of inflow items 1 to 9	407	1,164	201
Outflows			
1. Loans made	200	415[n]	112
2. Investments	80[p]	0	0
3. Equity capital withdrawn	0	0	0
4. Deposits withdrawn	0	5	16
5. Other borrowing repaid	110	209	0
6. Sale of farm inputs, consumer goods, and farm produce	0	170	0
7. Bad and doubtful debts	4[q]	0[r]	4[s]
8. Interest paid on deposits	0	5[t]	3[u]
9. Interest paid on other borrowings	20[v]	33[w]	0
10. Transaction costs	11	11	11
11. Sum of outflow items 1 to 10	425	843	146
12. Net inflow (+)/outflow (−) (that is, inflow item 10 *minus* outflow item 11)	−18	+321	+55
13. Profit (+)/loss (−) (that is, inflow items 7-9 *minus* outflow items 8-10)	−14	+21	+13
14. Unit transaction costs (percent)	1.41	0.67	3.16

[a]Scenario I is a base scenario in which the functional structure of a rural financial institution (RFI) system is unifunctional, with an annual interest rate on deposits of 5 percent, on other borrowings of 10 percent, and on farm-level loans of 12 percent.

[b]In scenario II, an RFI system is vertically and horizontally integrated, with annual interest rates on deposits of 5 percent, on other borrowings for making farm-level loans of 10 percent, for undertaking nonlending activities of 14 percent, and on farm-level loans of 12 percent.

(continued)

Table 55—Continued

[c]In scenario III, an RFI system is unifunctional, with revised annual interest rates on deposits of 10 percent, on other borrowings of 20 percent, and on farm-level loans of 24 percent.
[d]Assumed to result from a functional structure that is vertically as well as horizontally integrated.
[e]Assuming a 200 percent increase in the interest rate on deposits and an interest rate elasticity of deposits of 0.16 percent for India. Note that this is much higher than in Taiwan, but about one-half lower than in the U.S. farm sector.
[f]Other borrowings are not required, because new level of farm-level loan demand declines to $112 million, which can be financed from deposits, equity, and reserves. Farm-level loan demand declines because of the 200 percent increase in the interest rate on such loans, and because this demand elasticity with respect to the interest rate is −1.33 in the mid-1980s in India.
[g]Assumed to be 55 percent of loans made, as in India.
[h]Assumed to be 95 percent of loans made, as in Taiwan.
[i]Assumed to be 55 percent of loans made, as in India.
[j]Assumed to be 12 percent on inflow item 6 and 5 percent on outflow item 2.
[k]Assumed to be 12 percent on loans made.
[l]Assumed to be 24 percent on loans made.
[m]Assumed to be 12 percent on sale of farm inputs, consumer goods, farm produce, and so forth.
[n]Assumed to be made from equity, reserves, deposits, and other borrowings.
[p]Equity capital and reserves are invested as deposits with other banks or the treasury.
[q]Assumed to be 2 percent of loans made.
[r]Assumed to be negligible.
[s]Assumed to be 2 percent of loans made.
[t]Assumed to be 5 percent on deposits collected.
[u]Assumed to be 10 percent on deposits collected.
[v]Assumed to be 10 percent on other borrowings.
[w]Assumed to be 10 percent on other borrowings of $220 million for making farm-level loans and 14 percent on the rest of the other borrowings.

Under the base scenario, the RFI system is a net drain on public resources because it has a negative net inflow (−US$18 million) and net loss (−US$14 million). This largely results from its unifunctional structure; it concentrates on making farm-level loans and recovering them, aside from some minor equity collection and other borrowing functions. Under scenario II, the RFI becomes a net contributor, with a positive net inflow (US$321 million), profit (US$21 million), and unit transaction costs reduced to 0.67 percent.

The corresponding values under scenario III are US$55 million, US$13 million, and 3.16 percent—considerably less favorable than those under scenario II. Raising interest rates in this scenario does improve the performance of an RFI system over that in scenario I, but it is clearly not better than that under scenario II. This is because the scale and scope of operations under scenario III are smaller and narrower. Such operations do not improve loan repayment capacity and consequent loan recoveries and deposit collections. In addition, possible scale economies in transaction costs are reduced, and the RFI system's contribution to agricultural development is limited.

This hypothetical exercise shows that public policy should aim at building a relevant and robust RFI system, together with setting interest rates that are conducive to achieving the threefold fundamental objectives. Such a policy requires promotion of a vertically and horizontally integrated RFI system. Sustained and disciplined integrated institutional credit of this type has the potential to reduce the interest rates of informal lenders, a rate that decreased by 25 percent over two decades following 1951 in 13 developing countries, including Nigeria in Africa; India, Indonesia, Pakistan, the Philippines, South Vietnam, Sri Lanka, and Thailand in Asia; Colombia, Honduras, and Mexico in Latin America and the Caribbean; and Jordan and Lebanon in the Middle East (Wai 1972).

10

Conclusions
and Implications

Based on this review of the literature, it appears that agricultural credit policy in most countries in the world aims to facilitate rural growth with equity, integrate rural financial markets, and enlarge the economies of scale and scope for viability of formal RFIs, that is, public and private lending institutions such as commercial banks. Lessons learned from the cross-national analysis indicate that two main instruments required for achieving these goals are promoting appropriate RFIs and maintaining interest rates that are conducive to the fulfillment of these goals. These policies to develop RFIs have worked best in the context of new technology that reduces the cost of production per unit of output. Such policies follow an approach to the development of RFIs wherein supply interacts with demand. This is indeed different from supply-leading and demand-following approaches.

Modern forms of capital and an efficient capital market influence not only prices but also growth and employment. Rural financial market development is a complex process. This is because agriculture is small-scale, geographically widely dispersed, weather-dependent, highly complementary in its production process, only partially commercialized, and deprived of basic infrastructure and education. It is also because in developing countries rural loan demand is more elastic to the real interest rate than rural savings in general and rural financial deposits in particular. But the borrowing, saving, and deposit responses of rural households to the availability of accessible and appropriate RFIs are elastic. Thus, a widespread system of rural branches is important.

In these circumstances, there are limits to how much interest rates can be raised to improve the margins for RFIs. Similarly, in the early period of development of these institutions, there may be scale diseconomies. These suggest that promotion of a vertically and horizontally integrated formal RFI system is necessary because such a system has the potential to reap scale and scope economies, besides achieving the two other objectives: rural growth with equity and integration of rural financial markets. Further, in many countries, government support takes the form of contributions to equity capital, rediscounting facilities, administered interest rates, and credit and deposit insurance guarantees. While such support is common, the policy attention paid to promoting appropriate RFIs is limited and unsustained. The only major exceptions are Japan, Taiwan, the Republic of Korea, and the United States, where RFI systems are successful.

A developing rural credit system may be subject to political abuse because of its dispersed character, the nature of rural politics, and inappropriate interest rate policies. As a consequence, loan quality may be poor and loan delinquency widespread. However, other reasons for the viability problem of rural credit institutions are far more important. They relate more directly to inappropriate features of the policy of promoting formal institutions than to interest rates. A more appropriate strategy for development of RFIs, stressing developing multiple financial agencies that are functionally and vertically integrated, with high coverage of farmers and geographic areas, is outlined here, but no attempt is made to prepare a blueprint of prescriptions. This is so for both the instruments to promote appropriate formal RFIs and to maintain interest rates conducive to larger private investment, higher growth, and less inflation. On the former, the blueprint is not prepared because institution-building is a highly country- and situation-specific socio-political-economic phenomenon. What is attempted here is to delineate various organizing principles and discuss their implications to the promotion of appropriate RFIs. Similarly, no attempt is made to estimate a particular level of interest rate on rural loans or deposits.

Instead, three considerations are suggested for maintaining conducive interest rates. These are (1) expected rate of return on investment in agriculture, (2) the potential for reaping scale economies in transaction and other costs of RFIs, and (3) the normal inflation rate. The first encourages demand for and supply of loanable funds to accelerate private investment in agriculture, which is consistent with the developmental objectives. The second consideration implies that the level of interest rates should take into account the potential for reaping scale and scope economies by RFIs. And the third permits reasonable protection from erosion in the value of loanable funds and capital due to price-level changes, though interest rates may not be rigidly indexed to these changes. Thus, the higher the expected rate of return on investment in agriculture and the higher the inflation rate, the higher would be interest rates. But, as scale economies in the costs of RFIs are realized, the lower would be these rates. High rates of return to investment can accommodate higher interest rates where transaction costs are high, but as the transaction costs come down, so should the interest rates. Interest rates must be set to reflect these conditions. Pursuit of these three points would ensure that interest rates are set and demand for and supply of loanable funds are encouraged consistent with developmental objectives, and that the minimum point on the average/marginal cost curve of RFIs is reached.

Promoting Appropriate Formal Institutions

Nationally integrated RFIs are necessary and desirable for accomplishing financial intermediation between surplus and deficit seasons, years, regions, and economic subsystems. The rationale for developing RFIs is straightforward. The reasons are the advantages of monetization; the differential increase in demand for and supply of capital induced by widely dispersed agriculture with uneven availability of new technology; the problems arising from weather instability and low and static incomes of farmers; the financial requirements for land reforms and redemption of old debt during calamities; and the weaknesses of informal lenders. Moreover, historical patterns of economic development in both low- and high-income countries show that formal lenders have played an increasingly large role relative to informal lenders. There has been a strong secular increase in the relative role of institutional credit and a consequent decline in noninstitutional credit in Asian high-, middle-, and low-income countries. Cross-national data on various countries in six different geographical regions suggest a similar conclusion. The share of institutional loans in total loans to farmers was 28 percent in South Asia, 33 percent in Southeast Asia (excluding the Republic of Korea and Taiwan), 65 percent in the Near East and Mediterranean Basin, and 85 percent in Latin America and the Caribbean. The corresponding number for developed countries like Japan, the United States, the Republic of Korea, and Taiwan was more than 85 percent.

Given the rationale for RFIs on both deductive and inductive grounds, how should their development be structured? There are six organizing principles that need to be considered. First, should there be only one RFI or more than one? Although, there is little or no empirical evidence on duplication of loans for the same purpose, logic and observation favor a multiagency approach that provides a choice to farmers. Because RFIs have major problems with economy of scale, a large number of competing agencies may be undesirable. However, unlike the single agency, a multiagency approach has the potential to generate competition. Other reasons for a multiagency approach are shifts in the term structure of demand for and supply of financial services; the lack of comparative advantage of the existing RFIs due to the ill-suited term structure of their financial resources and their inability to serve the rural poor, especially in more difficult agricultural areas; and increasing availability of trained manpower over time. Historical experiences of countries around the world show that the multiagency approach is common in both developed and developing countries. The average absolute number of different types of RFIs is higher in high- and middle-income countries than in low-income countries in all the major regions of the world.

The second organizing principle relates to the form of organization of rural financial institutions, that is, should they be government departments, autonomous public agencies, private agencies, or cooperatives? There is no a priori reason for any one of them to perform better than the others. Moreover, historical experience shows that all these forms are found world over. But the process of promoting RFIs typically begins with government departments or cooperatives because commercial banks are reluctant to enter the rural financial markets—perhaps largely due to initial problems of scale and the difficulty of supervising widely dispersed small branches. In the process of rural financial market development, other forms of organization also emerge. Nevertheless, government programs are ubiquitous even in the later stage of development as in Japan, the United States, Taiwan, and the Republic of Korea. But they are well-integrated with the rest of the formal RFIs, which are government-supported autonomous banks or corporations, cooperatives, and private commercial banks.

The third important organizing principle for RFIs is vertical integration. Vertically organized RFIs are needed because they are capable of integrating national and regional financial markets, providing human know-how to lower-level units, and decentralizing decisions on rural financial operations. Such capability is weak in Sub-Saharan Africa, the Near East and Mediterranean Basin, and Latin America and the Caribbean, compared with Asia. The proportion of RFIs that are not vertically organized is higher in Africa, followed by Latin America and the Caribbean, the Near East and Mediterranean Basin, and then in Asia, excluding Japan, the Republic of Korea, and Taiwan, where all RFIs are vertically organized.

The fourth organizing principle that the policy must address is the density of field-level offices of an RFI that should be promoted. Improving the density of RFIs (that is, the number of field-level offices of RFIs per 1,000 hectares of arable land) is also extremely important to the development of the rural financial market. Although scale economies may be adversely affected, increasing density is still important because it improves accessibility for both rural households and the formal lenders and lowers the transaction costs of borrowing for farmers. Increased density also enables intensification and widening of the coverage of farmers and the scope of operations to develop scale economies, which are crucial for spreading lenders' common transaction costs. Moreover, it facilitates effective competition with informal lenders. Density of RFIs was lowest in Africa, followed by the Near East and Mediterranean Basin, Latin America and the Caribbean, and finally Asia. Density was highest in Japan (4.6), followed by China (3.7), Taiwan (1.3), the Republic of Korea (1.1); India (0.7), two Southeast Asian middle-income countries (the Philippines and Thailand) (0.39), and four South Asian low-income countries (Bangladesh, Indonesia, Nepal, and Sri Lanka) (0.3).

The fifth organizing principle is whether to cover a larger number of farmers and other rural clients, which is necessary and desirable in order to achieve scale and scope economies. Wide coverage is also essential to achieving the other two objectives of agricultural credit policy: rural growth with equity and better integration of rural financial markets. Moreover, it is required to institutionalize rural credit and also rural financial savings. There is also a closely related need to cover such rural clients as farm input distributors, farm produce processors, and even stores that sell consumer goods and repair services. Data on coverage of these types of rural clients are not available, but coverage of farmers was lowest in Africa (7 percent), followed by the Near East and Mediterranean Basin (9 percent), Latin America and the Caribbean (18 percent), and Asia (24 percent). The share of small farmers in the total number of farmers reached by RFIs was also higher in Asia than in the other regions.

Sixth and finally, the RFIs should have multiproduct and diversified operations that are mutually reinforcing so that horizontal integration can be attained. Multifunctional RFIs directly and indirectly undertake operation of farm-level loans (both in cash and kind, and in short and longer terms for crop and other enterprises), extension, input sales, produce marketing, consumer goods sales, collection of deposits or share capital, other borrowings, and loan recovery. Not all RFIs have to be multifunctional in explicit and direct terms, nor is it feasible given the common history of both unifunctional and somewhat-multifunctional RFIs in a given country at a given time. For example, land development banks may not be able to lend for short periods nor undertake auxiliary services such as produce marketing directly. Similarly, government departments will not have comparative advantage in collecting deposits. But both of these RFIs can effectively coordinate with other RFIs and thereby indirectly become multifunctional. Among other RFIs, vertically organized (nonland) cooperatives can directly play a multifunctional role by promoting financial services for farm inputs sales, farm produce marketing, and consumer goods sales by their field-level constituents. RFIs, like commercial banks and specialized agricultural banks, can make available their financial services not only to farmers but also to farm input distributors, farm produce marketers, and consumer goods shopkeepers.

A multifunctional RFI system is advantageous for more than one reason. First, it facilitates promotion of both working and fixed capital, the optimum combination of which is necessary to exploit fully the potential of new technology.

Second, by making loans for dairy farming, sheep-rearing, fishery, forestry, and other rural sideline occupations, such a system promotes a diversified and more robust agriculture, in addition to reaping scale economies in its own transaction costs.

Third, farm-level credit acts as an impetus to investment in real resources, which must be matched by supplies, which in turn could be encouraged by loans to input and produce marketing agencies. Through these types of agricultural credit, RFIs can forge much-needed backward and forward linkages among agricultural production, agricultural input distribution, and agromarketing and processing subsystems. These linkages improve the efficiency of agricultural productivity and the economies of scale and scope, and thereby increase viability, besides promoting larger noninflationary production and saving linkages of agriculture.

Fourth, multifunctional RFIs will also accelerate the consumption linkages of technological change because they have a larger impact on rural incomes as a result of stronger and noninflationary production and saving linkages.

Fifth, such RFIs will be an effective alternative to informal lenders who undertake a range of functions. In most developing countries, informal private lenders' operations are characterized by horizontal integration of local commodity, land, labor, and credit markets.

Both horizontally and vertically organized RFIs are widely found in such countries as Japan, the United States, the Republic of Korea, and Taiwan. They are also found in developing countries—widely in China, and to some extent in other Asian countries such as Bangladesh, India, Malaysia, and Thailand, and to a much lesser extent elsewhere. The share of countries with unifunctional RFI systems is highest in Africa, followed by Latin America and the Caribbean, the Near East and Mediterranean Basin, and then Asia.

Transaction costs, as a percentage of all assets plus liabilities of RFIs, are lower where their density, coverage, and multifunctional roles are greater: they averaged 1.1 percent in Taiwan, 1.5 percent in the Republic of Korea, 1.7 percent in the Near East and Mediterranean Basin, 2.4 percent in Asian LICs, 2.8 percent in Latin American and Caribbean MICs, and 3.1 percent in African MICs.

A successful example of a diversified agency is the Grameen Bank of Bangladesh, which not only makes farm-level loans, but also lends to local agroprocessing businesses, paddy trading, and repair shop services. It also collects deposits, recovers loans, and borrows from other agencies. This bank has encouraged investment, employment, and occupational diversification, in addition to increasing incomes and lowering poverty among the rural poor. It has also achieved viability, high rates of loan recovery, scale economies in financial costs, and constant returns to scale in transaction costs. Its rural branches achieve scale economies in transaction costs within three years of their inception. Indeed, these branches have continued to enjoy scale economies in these costs even beyond Tk 5.5 million of business. Moreover, this bank has been an effective alternative to noninstitutional lenders whose operations are similar to those described earlier.

Regional Rural Banks (RRBs) in India have also to some extent diversified their operations in a manner similar to the Grameen Bank. In the late 1970s, they lowered their unit transaction costs and improved profitability. In a similar example, farmers under the purview of a multifunctional village cooperative in India have larger investments, more optimal allocation of resources, better technology, and higher productivity and incomes than those served by a less diversified village cooperative in the same agroclimatically backward area. Moreover, the multifunctional village cooperative fully recovered its loans and had lower unit transaction costs and higher profitability. A sample of mostly rural branches of the nationalized commercial banks in India enjoyed scale economies in transaction costs in the mid-1980s. These branches, however, suffered from scale diseconomies in costs when their operations were only about Rs 1 million, but they rapidly reaped scale economies once operations grew to about Rs 30 million. These economies, moreover, continued even beyond a volume of business of Rs 60 million.

Furthermore, the adoption rates of high-yielding varieties and agricultural productivity were higher and the loan delinquency rates were lower in states of India where the density of RFIs was higher. In these states, loans to farmers and those to input distribution agencies were also higher and more diversified, and village cooperatives were multifunctional and achieved scale economies in their transaction costs.

In India, fertilizer use, irrigation, other agricultural investments, and agricultural productivity have increased over time, with the increase not only in the density of RFIs and farm-level credit, but also in loans for distribution of agricultural inputs, cooperative marketing of produce, and processing agencies. Nevertheless, at the all-India level, loan delinquency is high and scale economies in transaction costs have not been fully achieved. Had the institutions sustained increases in their density, coverage of farmers, scale and scope of farm-level loans, and multiproduct operations more continuously, institutional credit would have had a much larger impact on agricultural investments and productivity, profitability, and loan recoveries.

The sustained and disciplined integrated institutional credit described can further lower already-declining interest rates of informal lenders. This rate decreased by 25 percent over two decades from 1951 in 13 developing countries spread over Sub-Saharan Africa, Asia, Latin America and the Caribbean, and the Near East and Mediterranean Basin.

Determining the Level of Interest Rates

Interest rate policy formulation is perhaps even more complex than promotion of formal RFIs. Most transaction costs of an RFI are shared jointly by its various activities, including credit. The spread between borrowing and lending rates for agriculture is not the only source of revenue for RFIs. Other sources include the interest spread for other subsystems of agricultural development, commissions on nonfund-based credit, discounts on bills, check-clearing fees, and income from nonfinancial activities. Moreover, development policy aims to evolve a full set of viable intermediaries rather than a single activity like credit or deposit mobilization.

Viability of an RFI should be looked at in the broad context of its many activities, not just in terms of a single activity such as margins on lending. Furthermore, raising borrowing rates in isolation from lending rates tends to act as a disincentive to RFIs without promoting significant growth in rural deposits. Similarly, raising lending rates in isolation from deposit rates acts as a disincentive to rural borrowers, which is eventually counterproductive to the basic goals of a rural financial system.

The reasons for concern about interest rates that are too high or too low are clear. On a macroeconomic level, raising lending and deposit rates can lead to cost-push inflation, lower growth and saving rates, and bankruptcy, as was found in recent financial reforms in the Republic of Korea, Brazil, Chile, and Turkey. At the sectoral level, loan demand decreases more than proportionately in response to increases in the lending rate in developing countries, unlike developed countries; interest rate elasticity being -0.25 to -1.98 (with an average of -1.31) in the former group of countries as against -0.10 in the United States. Moreover, the interest rate has a greater impact on rural loan demand than on the supply of rural savings (with elasticities of 0.0005-0.50), and rural deposits (with elasticities of 0.002-0.16) in developing countries, compared with developed countries (with elasticities of 0.33-0.87). Therefore, raising interest rates excessively in the developing phase will tend to choke off rural loan demand without inducing substantial new financial deposits. In addition to the direct negative effect on economic activity, the adverse effect on growth in rural loans will retard development of scale economies in transaction costs of the RFIs.

A feeble response of rural deposits to interest rates is in significant part due to farmers' preference for holding their savings and assets in physical productive resources rather than in financial deposits. Even in developed countries, the share of such resources in total savings and assets is still very large. Furthermore, the interest rate is a less important determinant of both rural loan demand and rural deposit supply than nonprice factors in developing, as well as developed, countries. In developing countries, these factors mainly include the existence of new technology, the density of formal RFIs, and their multiproduct services. In addition to the last two factors, the safety and liquidity of these institutions' deposit facilities largely determine the supply of rural deposits in these countries.

Whether total rural saving (physical plus financial) will increase or decrease with the increase in the real interest rate cannot be stated a priori because of its positive substitution and possibly negative income effects. Empirical evidence on farm households in an Indian district, Taiwan, and the Republic of Korea shows that this response is positive but inelastic. This is due to a very high positive substitution effect of the rate of return, which has more than offset the possible negative income effect or has been reinforced by this impact also being positive. Such a result may have been induced by rapid and widespread technological change in agriculture. Moreover, rural saving is also influenced more by factors other than the rate of return. Most of these noninterest factors center around some measure of the ability to save.

Finally, promotion of a vertically and horizontally integrated RFI system has a much larger impact on its net contribution to public resources, compared with the effects of increases in interest rates on rural loans and rural deposits. Such a system can be designed by deliberately promoting financial services (viable loans, nonfund-based credit, collection of deposits and equity capital, legitimate refinancing, and so on), not only for the agricultural production subsystem, but also for farm inputs marketing, agromarketing and processing, and related rural sideline economic subsystems. It can also be designed by organizing educational and training programs for building such a system. That public goods like rural roads, transportation, electricity, and health and educational facilities must be developed is self-explanatory, but no country waits until these public goods are developed and until perfect macroeconomic management arises for an RFI system to emerge by itself, as historical patterns have shown. A more prudent policy approach is to simultaneously develop both the public goods and RFIs that serve the interests of their clients as well as themselves.

In conclusion, it is proposed that future research should especially address the following questions: What are the administrative costs for all activities between the original saver and the ultimate investor? What is the loan delinquency rate? How much of this is bad and doubtful debt? What is the viability of an institution after allowing for the cost of such debt?

For developing countries, three implications can be drawn for the development of formal RFIs. First, promotion of a nationally integrated formal rural financial market with sustained government support is essential to transfer of new technology for agricultural development. Second, in so doing, improvements in vertical organization, density, proportion of rural clients reached, and the functional structure of formal RFIs are central to their clients well-being and to their own. And third, these improvements, together with the maintenance of conducive interest rates, are far more important to achieving the objectives than financial liberalization alone. Such liberalization may be important, but to be effective, it must be accompanied by the positive actions stated here.

Appendix 1
Methodology

Proof that Equations (14) and (15) are the Same

Let the estimated two variable multiple regression be

$$\hat{Y} = a + \hat{\beta}_1 X_1 + \hat{\beta}_2 X_2 + E_1 . \tag{1}$$

Let

$$x_1 = X_1 - \bar{X}_1 ,$$

$$x_2 = X_2 - \bar{X}_2 ,$$

$$y = Y - \bar{Y}, \text{ and}$$

$$x_1 x_2 = (X_1 - \bar{X}_1)(X_2 - \bar{X}_1).$$

$$\hat{\beta}_1 = \frac{(\Sigma x_2^2)(\Sigma x_1 y) - (\Sigma x_1 x_2)(\Sigma x_2 y)}{(\Sigma x_1^2)(\Sigma x_2^2) - (\Sigma x_1 x_2)^2} , \text{ and} \tag{2}$$

$$\hat{\beta}_2 = \frac{(\Sigma x_1^2)(\Sigma x_2 y) - (\Sigma x_1 x_2)(\Sigma x_1 y)}{(\Sigma x_1^2)(\Sigma x_2^2) - (\Sigma x_1 x_2)^2} . \tag{3}$$

Let

$$\sigma^2 = \Sigma(Y - \hat{y})^2 / n - k,$$

where k is the number of parameters estimated and $Y - \hat{y}$ is the measure of the failure of the X's to predict Y.

The standard error of

$$\hat{\beta}_1 = se(\hat{\beta}_1) = \sigma \sqrt{\Sigma x_2^2 / [(\Sigma x_1^2)(\Sigma x_2^2) - (\Sigma x_1 x_2)^2]} , \text{ and} \tag{4}$$

The standard error of

$$\hat{\beta}_2 = se\,(\hat{\beta}_2) = \sigma\,\sqrt{\Sigma x_1^2\,/\,[(\Sigma x_1^2)\,(\Sigma x_2^2) - (\Sigma x_1 x_2)^2]}\;. \tag{5}$$

$$t_1 = \hat{\beta}_1/se(\hat{\beta}_1)\,. \tag{6}$$

$$t_2 = \hat{\beta}_2/se(\hat{\beta}_2)\,. \tag{7}$$

The standard ∂ coefficient is

$$\hat{\beta}_1^\star = \hat{\beta}_1 x\,\sqrt{\frac{\Sigma x_1^2}{\Sigma y^2}}\;,\ \ \text{and} \tag{8}$$

The standard ∂ coefficient is

$$\hat{\beta}_2^\star = \hat{\beta}_2 x\,\sqrt{\frac{\Sigma x_2^2}{\Sigma y^2}}\;. \tag{9}$$

$$\hat{\beta}_1^\star = t_1 \cdot se\,(\hat{\beta}_1)\,\sqrt{\frac{\Sigma x_1^2}{\Sigma y^2}}\;, \tag{10}$$

since

$$\hat{\beta}_1 = t_1 \cdot se\,(\hat{\beta}_1)\,,\ \ \text{and}$$

$$\hat{\beta}_2^\star = t_2 \cdot se\,(\hat{\beta}_2)\,\sqrt{\frac{\Sigma x_2^2}{\Sigma y^2}}\;, \tag{11}$$

since

$$\hat{\beta}_2 = t_2 \cdot se\,(\hat{\beta}_2)\,.$$

Substituting the formula for *se* $(\hat{\beta}_1)$ from equation (4) in (10),

$$\hat{\beta}_1^* = t_1 \cdot \sigma \sqrt{(\Sigma x_2^2 / [(\Sigma x_1^2)(\Sigma x_2^2) - (\Sigma x_1 x_2)^2])} \times \sqrt{\frac{\Sigma x_1^2}{\Sigma y^2}} \ . \tag{12}$$

Substituting the formula for *se* $(\hat{\beta}_2)$ from equation (5) in (11),

$$\hat{\beta}_2^* = t_2 \cdot \sigma \sqrt{\Sigma x_1^2 / [(\Sigma x_1^2)(\Sigma x_2^2) - (\Sigma x_1 x_2)^2]} \times \sqrt{\frac{\Sigma x_2^2}{\Sigma y^2}} \ . \tag{13}$$

$$\hat{\beta}_1^* = t_1 \cdot \sigma \sqrt{\frac{(\Sigma x_2^2)(\Sigma x_1^2)}{(\Sigma x_1^2)(\Sigma x_2^2) - (\Sigma x_1 x_2)^2}} \times \frac{1}{\sqrt{\Sigma y^2}} \ , \text{ and} \tag{14}$$

$$\hat{\beta}_2^* = t_2 \cdot \sigma \sqrt{\frac{(\Sigma x_1^2)(\Sigma x_2^2)}{(\Sigma x_1^2)(\Sigma x_2^2) - (\Sigma x_1 x_2)^2}} \times \frac{1}{\sqrt{\Sigma y^2}} \ . \tag{15}$$

Therefore, equations (14) and (15) are equivalent.

Appendix 2

Reasons for Delinquency in Repayment of Agricultural Loans in Selected Countries

Region/Country	Reason
High delinquency	
Sub-Saharan Africa	
Low-income countries	
Ethiopia, Chilalo	Loan program expanded rapidly; failure to take first defaulters to court on account of lack of full support and cooperation of local institutions; requirement of down payment for loans; profitability of cereals lower than expected due to declining prices; lack of consumption credit.
Ethiopia, Minimum Package Programme (MPP)	Requirement of down payment for loans; lower than expected profitability on cereals due to declining prices; lack of consumption credit.
Upper Volta	Delay in loan sanction; low crop yield; adverse weather; delay in getting animal traction package.
Middle-income countries	
Kenya, the Vihiga	Improper identification of farmers who did not really need credit; lower than expected profitability of the maize enterprise because of inadequate credit for hiring labor for land preparation and more than adequate credit for fertilizers.
Asia	
Low-income countries	
Bangladesh	Unsound lending; inadequate supervision; natural calamities; diversion of loans; unwillingness to repay.
India	Failure to tie up lending with development programs and with productive investment; ineffective, unrealistic, and faulty loan recovery policies; lack of market tie-ups including that for inputs; lack of supervision; delayed loan

Region/Country	Reason
	disbursement; overfinancing or underfinancing; apathy and indifference of bank management; lack of discipline and responsibility among borrowers.
Indonesia	Vagaries of weather; price fluctuations; speculative borrowing; under BIMAS program, crop damage; lack of incentives to repay; ineffective collection efforts.
Nepal	Lack of irrigation and support services; dependence on weather; deliberate nonrepayment because no action may be taken by the bank (ADB's findings).
Pakistan	Improper assessment of loan requirement; natural calamities; lack of supervision; poor collection efforts; improper farm technology; socioeconomic factors.
Sri Lanka	Seasonal factors (income variation due to seasonal factors); defects in credit delivery system; crop failure; misallocation of borrowed funds.
Middle-income countries China, People's Republic of	Poor material benefits on the loan.
Korea, Republic of	Poor loan supervision; sociopolitical power; natural calamities.
Malaysia	Limited follow-up.
Philippines	Calamities; poor market prices; ineffective collection efforts; lack of capacity to pay.
Taiwan	Lack of attention in recovery; inappropriate handling of loan duration; lack of working experience; interference of the "ultraleftists"; natural calamities.
Thailand	Emergency; legal action/confiscation of property; crop damage; too much outside debt; intentional defaults (in that order of importance); inability to repay loans.
Latin America and the Caribbean Middle-income countries Brazil	Concept of loan repayment being unfamiliar (particularly for government loans); collateral not required; low subsidized interest rate; poor asset quality, which arises from related lending to firms within a conglomerate.
Chile	Same as above.

Region/Country	Reason
Near East and Mediterranean Basin **Middle-income countries** Yemen, Republic of	Shortage of rainfall; depletion of watertable in wells; inappropriate repayment schedule; insufficiency of loan given; failure to implement the project on account of nonavailability of supplies at the market; lack of production facilities (poultry); borrower delays.
Jordan	Drought; poor administration and technical efficiency; poor supporting services like extension and marketing.
Low delinquency **Sub-Saharan Africa** **Low-income country** Ethiopia, Wolamo Agricultural Development Unit (WADU)	No requirement for down payment for loans; extension of consumption credit at low interest rate; profitable investment, especially in coffee, which brought higher prices than cereals; higher willingness of borrowers to repay loans in time; this desire was reinforced by WADU's policy, followed from the outset, of excluding all farmers from a given area from future credit programs if repayment for the area fell below 95 percent.
Near East and Mediterranean Basin **Middle-income countries** Egypt	Creation of banks closer to farmers; credit in kind; increased administrative efficiency through training program; availability of irrigation/water throughout the year; smooth availability of marketing facilities for both farm inputs and products.
Jordan	Institutional laws do not approve of any interest or capital exemptions; borrowers are notified almost two months in advance; borrowers have option to repay their maturing debts by authorizing Jordan company for marketing and manufacturing agricultural products to repay.
Syria	Farmers are interested in keeping their credit rating; effective loan appraisal and supervision; effective loan recovery apparatus; high coordination among cooperatives, marketing institutions, and banks; loan recovery through produce marketing by public-sector marketing institutions through the bank; fear of foreclosure; fees and prohibition from attaining further loans;incentives to loan collectors; par-

Region/Country	Reason
	ticipation of farmers' union and administrative authorities in promoting high loan recoveries; stringent measures are applied in supervising the implementation of the agricultural productivity plan.
North America High-income country United States	Diversity of lenders; suitable lending terms and techniques; very favorable past loan repayment records.
Latin America and the Caribbean All countries in general	Large proportion of loans are collateralized; large proportion of loans are refinanced, rephased, and rescheduled; large proportion of loans are given to larger farmers; small coverage of farmers both in absolute and relative terms; regular loan repayers are guaranteed continuation of credit line even if others do not repay; low interest rate on agricultural loans compared to nonagricultural; more professional lending decisions and decentralized with the involvement of the local farmers; deprivation of loans for new crops as well as new borrowers; diversion of institutional credit to other uses from which loans are repaid.
Asia	Differences in loan delinquencies
All countries in general	Degree of progressiveness of farmers; geographical conditions affecting agricultural productivity; tenurial arrangements; sociocultural realities; and degree of efficiency of the lending institution.

Sources: Agabin 1988b; Asian Development Bank 1985; Asian Productivity Organization 1984; FAO 1973; Lele 1975; NENARCA 1987; Olin 1975; and Onchon 1982.

References

Abbott, J. C. 1973a. Agricultural credit: Institutions and performance with particular reference to the Near East. *Monthly Bulletin of Agricultural Economics and Statistics* 20 (2): 1-12.

———. 1973b. Credit institutions and their impact on agricultural development in Africa. *Monthly Bulletin of Agricultural Economics and Statistics* 20 (10-11).

Adams, D. W. 1977. Policy issues in rural finance and development. Paper presented at a conference on rural finance research, sponsored by the Agricultural Development Council, the American Agricultural Economics Association, and the Ohio State University, 28 July to 1 August, San Diego, California.

———. 1978. Mobilizing household savings through rural financial markets. *Economic Development and Cultural Change* 26 (3): 547-560.

———. 1979. Borrowing costs and the demand for rural credit. *Journal of Development Studies* 15 (2): 165-176.

———. 1980. Recent performance of rural financial markets. In *Borrowers and lenders: Rural financial markets and institutions in developing countries*, ed. J. Howell, 15-33. London: Overseas Development Institute.

———. 1988a. The conundrum of successful credit projects in floundering rural financial markets. *Economic Development and Cultural Change* 36 (2): 355-367.

———. 1988b. Distinctive features of rural financial markets in Asia. In *Farm finance and agricultural development*. Tokyo: Asian Productivity Organization.

Adams, D., and Y. Kato. 1978. *Research on rural finance: A seminar report*. Report No. 17. New York: Agricultural Development Council.

Adams, D., and G. I. Nehman. 1976. Interest rates, borrowing costs, and agricultural loan demand. Ohio State University, Department of Agricultural Economics and Rural Sociology, Columbus, Ohio, U.S.A. Mimeo.

Adams, D., and J. L. Tommy. 1972. Financing small farms: The Brazilian experience 1965-69. Ohio State University, Department of Agricultural Economics and Rural Sociology, Columbus, Ohio, U.S.A. Mimeo.

Adams, D., C.-Y. Ahn, and K.-N. Hyun. 1977. Rural household savings in South Korea: 1963-1974. *Farm Management Notes for Asia and the Far East*, Regional Issue No. 4.

Adams, D., D. J. Graham, and J. D. Von Pischke, eds. 1984. *Undermining rural development with cheap credit*. Boulder, Colo., U.S.A.: Westview Press.

Adeyemo, R. 1984. Loan delinquency in multi-purpose cooperative union in Kwara State, Nigeria. *Savings and Development* 8 (3): 267-274.

Agabin, M. H. 1985. Philippines. In *Farm credit in selected Asian countries*, 146-156. Tokyo: Asian Productivity Organization.

_____. 1987. Rural savings mobilization: Asian perspective. In *Farm finance and agricultural development*, 81-109. Tokyo: Agricultural Productivity Organization.

_____. 1988a. Farm loan default: Philippine perspective. In *Farm finance and agricultural development*, 247-265. Tokyo: Agricultural Productivity Organization.

_____. 1988b. Government policies on agricultural credit in Asia. In *Farm finance and agricultural development*, 269-313. Tokyo: Agricultural Productivity Organization.

Agricultural Finance Corporation. 1988. Role and effectiveness of lending institutions. Draft Report, vol. 3. Bombay, India.

Ahmed, A. H. 1980. *Lender behaviour and the recent performance of rural financial markets in the Sudan*. Ann Arbor, Mich., U.S.A.: University Microfilms International.

Ahmed, A. H., and D. W. Adams. 1987. Transaction costs in Sudan's rural financial market. *African Review of Money, Finance, and Banking* 11 (January): 1-13.

Ahmed, S. El-M. 1977. The integration of agricultural credit and marketing in the Gezira Scheme of the Sudan, with special reference to the 'Shail System'. Ph.D. diss., Wye College, University of London, U.K.

Ahn, C. Y., D. W. Adams, and Y. K. Ro. 1979. Rural household savings in the Republic of Korea, 1962-1976. *Journal of Economic Development* 4 (1): 53-75.

Akompong, K. 1976. The effect of interest rate on the operations of rural credit—savings activities. Bank of Ghana, Accra. Mimeo.

Aku, P. S. 1986. Lending to farmers through the commercial banks in a developing economy: The Nigerian experience. *Agricultural Systems* 22 (1): 23-32.

Alamgir, M. 1976. Rural savings and investment in developing countries: Some conceptual and empirical issues. *Bangladesh Development Studies* 4 (1): 1-48.

American Bankers Association. 1983. *Commercial banks and the cooperative farm credit system: Institutional structure for a competitive environment.* Washington, D.C.

APRACA (Asian and Pacific Regional Agricultural Credit Association). 1983. *Agricultural credit policies and programmes in Asia (with special reference to small farmer development): Country profiles 1982 and strategy for recovery of loans.* Bangkok: FAO Regional Office for Asia and the Pacific.

APRACA/ESCAP Group Study/Observation Programme. 1984. *Agricultural credit and banking system in China.* APRACA No. 12. Bangkok, Thailand: Asian and Pacific Regional Agricultural Credit Association and the Economic and Social Commission for Asia and the Pacific (FAO Regional Office for Asia and the Pacific).

Araujo, P. F. C. 1967. An economic study of factors affecting the demand for agricultural credit at the farm level. M.S. thesis, Ohio State University, Columbus, Ohio, U.S.A.

Araujo, P. F. C., and R. L. Meyer. 1977. Agricultural credit policy in Brazil: Objectives and results. *American Journal of Agricultural Economics* 59 (5): 957-961.

Argyle, B. D. 1983. Development assistance, national policies, and lender type and performance. In *Rural financial markets in developing countries*, ed. J. D. Von Pischke, D. W. Adams, and G. Donald, 330-335. Baltimore, Md., U.S.A.: Johns Hopkins University Press.

Asian Development Bank. 1985. *Improving domestic resource mobilization through financial development.* Manila, Philippines: ADB.

Asian Productivity Organization. 1984. *Farm credit situation in Asia.* Tokyo: APO.

_____. 1985. *Farm credit in selected Asian countries.* Tokyo: APO.

_____. 1988. *Farm finance and agricultural development.* Tokyo: APO.

Baird, A. 1978. Extension and credit in an integrated rural development project in Sierra Leone. *Institute of Development Studies Bulletin* 1 (1).

140

Baker, C. B., and V. K. Bhargava. 1974. Financing small farm development in India. *Australian Journal of Agricultural Economics* 18 (2): 101-118.

Bank of Korea. 1976. Interest rate and aggregate savings behaviour in Korea. *Quarterly Economic Review of the Bank of Korea* (March).

Bathrick, D., and G. G. Casco. 1983. Innovative approaches to agricultural credit in INVIERNO/PROCAMPO project in Nicaragua. In *Rural financial markets in developing countries*, ed. J. D. Von Pischke, D. W. Adams, and G. Donald, 206-211. Baltimore and London: Johns Hopkins University Press.

Bauer, C. K. 1952. Proceedings of the international conference on cooperative credit. Berkeley, Calif.

Belshaw, D. G. R. 1988a. Default incidence and loan recovery strategy in agricultural credit programmes: Experience in Sub-Saharan Africa. In *Farm finance and agricultural development*, 237-246. Tokyo: Agricultural Productivity Organization.

_____. 1988b. Roles and performance of financial markets and institutions in agricultural development in Africa. In *Farm finance and agricultural development*. Tokyo: Agricultural Productivity Organization.

Belshaw, H. 1959. *Agricultural credit in economically underdeveloped countries*. Rome: Food and Agriculture Organization of the United Nations.

Bhaduri, A. 1973. A study in agricultural backwardness under semi-feudalism. *Economic Journal* 83 (329): 120-137.

Bhatt, V. V. 1970. Some aspects of deposits mobilization. *Economic and Political Weekly*, September 5, 1495-1497.

_____. 1978. *Interest rate, transaction costs, and financial innovations*. Domestic Finance Study No. 47. Washington, D.C.: World Bank.

_____. 1983. Financial innovations and development. In *Rural financial markets in developing countries*, ed. J. D. Von Pischke, D. W. Adams, and G. Donald, 43-49. Baltimore, Md., U.S.A.: Johns Hopkins University Press.

Bhattacharya, K. 1978. Financial intermediation and rural development: Role of cooperative credit in agricultural development. *The Indian Economic Journal* 26 (2): 11-24.

Binswanger, H. P., S. R. Khandker, and M. R. Rosenzweig. 1989a. *Determinants and effects of the expansion of the financial system in rural India*. Washington, D.C.: World Bank.

_____. 1989b. How infrastructure and financial institutions affect agricultural output and investment in India. Latin America and

141

Caribbean Country Department II, WPS-163. Washington, D.C.: World Bank.

Blyn, G. 1976. Saving and consumption behaviour of Punjab cultivators: 1954/55 to 1964/65. *Indian Economic Journal* 24 (1): 50-71.

Boskin, M. J. 1978. Taxation, saving, and the rate of interest. *Journal of Political Economy* 86 (2, Part 2): S3-S27.

Bottomley, A. 1963. The costs of administering private loans in under-developed rural areas. *Oxford Economic Papers* 15 (2): 154-163.

Bottrall, A., and J. Howell. 1980. Small farmers credit delivery and institutional choice. In *Borrowers and lenders: Rural financial markets and institutions in developing countries*, ed. J. Howell, 141-166. London: Overseas Development Institute.

Brake, J. R. 1971. The credit delivery system in Korea. Department of Agricultural Economics, Michigan State University, Ann Arbor, Mich., U.S.A. Mimeo.

Brake, J. R., C. E. Frost, H. E. Larzelere, G. E. Rossmiller, J. D. Shaffer, and V. L. Sorenson. 1971. *The national agricultural cooperation federation: An appraisal*. Special Report No. 1. Korea and Ann Arbor, Mich., U.S.A.: Korean Agricultural Study, Agricultural Research Institute, Ministry of Agriculture and Forestry, Seoul, Korea, and Department of Agricultural Economics, Michigan State University.

Braun, J. von, and D. Puetz. 1987. An African fertilizer crisis: Origin and economic effects in The Gambia. *Food Policy* 12 (4): 337-348.

Braverman, A., and J. K. Guash. 1986. Rural credit markets and institutions in developing countries: Lessons for policy analysis from practice and modern theory. *World Development* 14 (10/11): 1253-1267.

Central Bank of Sri Lanka. Undated. Strategy for recovery of agricultural loans. Department of Rural Credit, Sri Lanka. Mimeo.

Central Union of Agricultural Cooperatives. 1971. *The purchasing activities of the agricultural cooperatives*. RECA Publication Series No. 5. Tokyo: Research and Education Centre of AARRO.

_____. 1980a. *The agricultural cooperatives in Japan*. Tokyo.

_____. 1980b. *Agricultural cooperative movement in Japan*. Tokyo.

Chand, R., and D. S. Sidhu. 1985. Characteristics of defaulters of agricultural credit in Punjab—A discriminant function approach. *Indian Cooperative Review* 22 (3): 251-262.

Chavez, J. J. R. 1983. Centralized rediscounting and loan guarantee facilities. In *Rural financial markets in developing countries*, ed. J. D.

Von Pischke, D. W. Adams, and G. Donald, 162-168. Baltimore, Md., U.S.A.: Johns Hopkins University Press.

Chidebelu, A. N., and K. N. Ezike. 1988. Agricultural development projects approach to smallholder credit: The case of Lifia agricultural development project, Nigeria. *Quarterly Journal of International Agriculture* 27 (2): 186-196.

Chu, C. H. 1988. Government policies on farm credit: The case of the Republic of Korea. In *Farm finance and agricultural development*, 332-342. Tokyo: Agricultural Productivity Organization.

Colyer, D., and G. Jimenez. 1971. Supervised credit as a tool in agricultural development. *American Journal of Agricultural Economics* 53 (4): 639-642.

Cuevas, C. E. 1984. Intermediation costs and scale economies of banking under financial regulation in Honduras. Ph.D. diss., Ohio State University, Columbus, Ohio, U.S.A.

_____. 1987a. Institutional credit in rural Niger: Low performance and high costs. Economic and Sociology Occasional Paper No. 1351. Department of Agricultural Economics and Rural Sociology, Ohio State University, Columbus, Ohio, U.S.A.

_____. 1987b. Transaction costs of agricultural lending in developing countries. Economic and Sociology Occasional Paper No. 1418. Department of Agricultural Economics and Rural Sociology, Ohio State University, Columbus, Ohio, U.S.A.

Cuevas, C. E., and D. H. Graham. 1984. Agricultural lending costs in Honduras. In *Undermining rural development with cheap credit*, ed. D. Adams, D. J. Graham, and J. D. Von Pischke, 96-103. Boulder, Colo., U.S.A.: Westview Press.

Dantwala, M. L. 1966. Institutional credit in subsistence agriculture. *International Journal of Agrarian Affairs* 5 (1).

David, C. C. 1979. Structure and performance of rural financial markets in the Philippines. Economic and Sociology Occasional Paper No. 589. Ohio State University, Columbus, Ohio, U.S.A.

David, C. C., and R. L. Meyer. 1983. Measuring the farm level impact of agricultural loans. In *Rural financial markets in developing countries*, ed. J. D. Von Pischke, D. W. Adams, and G. Donald, 84-95. Baltimore, Md., U.S.A.: Johns Hopkins University Press.

Day, R. H., and I. Singh. 1977. *Economic development as an adaptive process: The green revolution in the Indian Punjab.* Cambridge, U.K.: Cambridge University Press.

Deaton, A. 1989. *Saving in developing countries: Theory and review.* Research Programme in Development Studies Discussion Paper No.

144. Princeton, N.J., U.S.A.: Woodrow Wilson School, Princeton University.

de Guia, E. O. 1972. *A comparative study of fertilizer distribution systems in five developing countries*. Paris: OECD.

De Macedo, J. 1988. Comments on financial liberalization in retrospect: Interest rate policies in LDCs. In *The state of development economics: Progress and perspectives*, ed. R. Gustav and T. P. Schultz, 411-415. Oxford, U.K.: Basil Blackwell.

Desai, B. M. 1975. *Relationship of consumption and production in changing agriculture: A study in Surat District, India*. Technological Change in Agriculture Project, Discussion Paper No. 80. Ithaca, N.Y., U.S.A.: Cornell University.

_____. 1976. Formal and informal credit supply sources in tribal areas: A case of Dharmpur Taluka. *Arthavikas* 12 (2): 78-94.

_____. 1978. Viability and equity objectives of institutional credit for agriculture. In *Agricultural finance: Papers and proceedings of the seminar*, ed. D. Angrish. Junagadh, Gujarat, India: Gujarat Agricultural University.

_____. 1979. Rural banking in India: Its performance and problems. *Prajnan* 8 (2): 113-134.

_____. 1980. Delivery of credit to rural poor. In *Adaptation of development administration for rural development*. Bangkok: ESCAP of the United Nations.

_____. 1983a. Group lending in rural areas. In *Rural financial markets in developing countries*, ed. J. D. Von Pischke, D. W. Adams, and G. Donald, 284-288. Baltimore, Md., U.S.A.: Johns Hopkins University Press.

_____. 1983b. Research on rural savings in India. *Vikalpa* 8 (2): 135-145.

_____. 1986a. Credit: Summaries of group discussion. *Indian Journal of Agricultural Economics* 42 (1): 29-31.

_____. 1986b. Performance of group-based savings and credit programme in rural India. *Prajnan* 15 (2): 145-160.

_____. 1989. Objectives and role of institutional finance for agricultural and rural development. *Vikalpa* 14 (2): 25-33.

Desai, B. M., and N. V. Namboodiri. 1991. *Performance of institutional finance for agriculture in India*. New Delhi: Oxford and IBH Publishing.

Desai, B. M., and Y. N. Rao. 1978. Default of cooperative loans: Problems, causes, and a strategy for solution. *Prajnan* 7 (2): 167-178.

Desai, B. M., V. K. Gupta, and G. Singh. 1988. Institutional credit for green revolution areas under semi-arid tropics in India. *Indian Journal of Agricultural Economics* 43 (1): 1-13.

Desai, B. M., R. Gupta, and B. L. Tripathi. 1989. *Framework for an integrative role of rural financial institutions: A study of Malpur Taluka in Gujarat.* New Delhi: Oxford and IBH Publishing.

Desai, D. K. 1988. Institutional credit requirements for agricultural production—2000 AD. *Indian Journal of Agricultural Economics* 43 (3): 326-355.

Desai, V. V. 1978. Some aspects of farm loans by commercial banks. *Indian Journal of Agricultural Economics* 33 (4): 79-84.

D'Mello, L. 1980. Lending to small farmers: The Indian case. In *Borrowers and lenders: Rural financial markets and institutions in developing countries*, ed. J. Howell, 35-58. London: Overseas Development Institute.

Donald, G. 1976. *Credit for small farmers in developing countries.* Boulder, Colo., U.S.A.: Westview Press.

Egaitsu, F. 1988a. Farm finance and agricultural capital formation. In *Farm finance and agricultural development*, 155-172. Tokyo: Agricultural Productivity Organization.

_____. 1988b. Historical sketch of agriculture and farm finance. In *Farm finance and agricultural development*, 125-138. Tokyo: Agricultural Productivity Organization.

Eicher, C. K., and D. C. Baker. 1982. *Research on agricultural development in Sub-Saharan Africa: A critical survey.* International Development Paper No. 1. Ann Arbor, Mich., U.S.A.: Michigan State University.

Emery, R. F. 1970. *The financial institutions of Southeast Asia: A country-by-country study.* New York: Praeger.

Englemann, K. 1968. *Building cooperative movements in developing countries: The sociological and psychological aspects.* New York: Praeger.

FAO (Food and Agriculture Organization of the United Nations). 1973. *Agricultural credit for selected countries of the Near East Region and the Mediterranean Basin.* Report of a seminar held in Rome, Italy, 29 January - 9 February 1973. Rome: FAO.

_____. 1974a. *Agricultural credit for small farmers in Latin America.* Report of a seminar held in Quito, Ecuador, 25-30 November 1974. Rome: FAO.

_____. 1974b. *Agricultural credit in Africa.* Report of a seminar held in Accra, Ghana, 3-14 December 1973. Rome: FAO.

_____. 1975. *Agricultural credit in Asia*. Report of a seminar held in Bangkok, Thailand, 7-18 October 1974. Rome: FAO.

_____. 1976. *Agricultural credit in the Caribbean Area*. Report of a seminar held in Paramaribo, Surinam, 2-10 March 1976. Rome: FAO.

_____. 1980. *Central banks, agricultural credit, and rural development*. Rome: FAO.

Feder, G., L. J. Lau, J. Y. Lin, and L. Xiapong. 1989. Agricultural credit and farm performance in China. *Journal of Comparative Economics* 13 (4): 508-526.

Firth, R., and B. S. Yamey. 1964. *Capital, saving, and credit in peasant societies*. London: George Allen and Unwin.

Friend, I. 1963. Determinants of the volume and composition of saving with special reference to the influence of monetary policy. In *Impact of monetary policy: Commission on money and credit*. Englewood Cliffs, N.J., U.S.A.: Prentice-Hall.

Fry, M. 1978. Money and capital or financial deepening in economic development? *Journal of Money, Credit, and Banking* 10 (4): 464-475.

_____. 1980. Saving, investment, growth, and the cost of financial repression. *World Development* 8 (4): 317-327.

_____. 1988. *Money, interest, and banking in economic development*. Baltimore, Md., U.S.A.: Johns Hopkins University Press.

Gadgil, M. V. 1986. Agricultural credit in India: A review of performance and policies. *Indian Journal of Agricultural Economics* 41 (3): 282-309.

Galbraith, J. K. 1952. *A theory of price control*. Cambridge, Mass., U.S.A.: Harvard University Press.

Gheen, W. E. 1976. Development banks: Empirical derivation of the loan administration cost curve. Ph.D. diss., University of Maryland, College Park, Md., U.S.A.

Giovannini, A. 1983. The interest elasticity of savings in developing countries: The existing evidence. *World Development* 11 (7): 601-607.

_____. 1985. Saving and the real interest rate in LDCs. *Journal of Development Economics* 18 (2-3): 197-217.

Goldkowsky, R. 1978. Financial aspects of smallholder development with special reference to Kenya. In *Schriften der Gesellschaft für Wirtschafts-Sozialwissenschaften des Landbaus*. Munich/Vienna.

Goldsmith, R. W. 1969. *Financial structure and development*. New Haven, Conn., U.S.A.: Yale University Press.

Goltz, A., and D. Lachman. 1974. Monetary correction and Colombia's savings and loans system. *Finance and Development* 11 (3): 24-26.

Gonzalez-Vega, C. 1976. On the iron law of interest rate restrictions: Agricultural credit policies in Costa Rica and in other less developed countries. Ph.D. diss. Stanford University, Stanford, Calif., U.S.A.

———. 1986. Strengthening agricultural banking and credit systems in Latin America and the Caribbean. Economic and Sociology Occasional Paper 1256. Ohio State University, Columbus, Ohio, U.S.A.

Gothoskar, S. P. 1989. Some aspects of growth of banking in India. *Journal of Indian School of Political Economy* 1 (1): 84-113.

Gotsch, C. H., and S. Yusuf. 1975. Technical indivisibilities and distribution of income: A mixed integer programming model of Punjab agriculture. *Food Research Institute Studies* 14 (1): 81-98.

Graham, D. H. 1987. Towards the development of rural financial institutions in Africa: The lessons from Niger. Economic and Sociology Occasional Paper 1312. Ohio State University, Columbus, Ohio, U.S.A.

Graham, D. H., and C. Bourne. 1983. Agricultural credit and rural progress in Jamaica. In *Rural financial markets in developing countries*, ed. J. D. Von Pischke, D. W. Adams, and G. Donald, 190-199. Baltimore, Md., U.S.A.: Johns Hopkins University Press.

Green, G. J. B. 1983. The role of commercial banking in agriculture. In *Rural financial markets in developing countries*, ed. J. D. Von Pischke, D. W. Adams, and G. Donald, 155-161. Baltimore, Md., U.S.A.: Johns Hopkins University Press.

Gregory, G. L., and D. W. Adams. 1986. Severity of rural loan recovery problems in Bangladesh. Economic and Sociology Occasional Paper 1319. Ohio State University, Columbus, Ohio, U.S.A.

Gupta, A. K. 1985. Management of rural credit and support system: An organizational study of financial institutions in drought-prone districts. Ph.D. diss., Kurukshetra University, Kurukshetra, India.

Gupta, K. L. 1970a. Household savings in financial assets: A case study of India. *Indian Economic Journal* 17 (2): 500-514.

———. 1970b. On some determinants of rural and urban household saving behavior. *The Economic Record* 46 (116): 578-583.

———. 1970c. Personal saving in developing nations: Further evidence. *The Economic Record* 46 (114): 243-249.

Gurley, J. G., and E. S. Shaw. 1955. Financial aspects of economic development. *American Economic Review* 45 (4): 515-538.

_____. 1960. *Money in theory of finance*. Washington, D.C.: Brookings Institution.

Habibulah, B. 1982. Financial intermediation and rural economic development. *Bank Parikrama* 7 (3-4).

Hadiwegeno, S. S. 1974. Potential effects of modification in the credit program for small farms in East Java, Indonesia. Ph.D. diss., University of Illinois, Urbana, Ill., U.S.A.

Hamberger, M. J. 1968. Household demand for financial assets. *Econometrica* 36 (1).

Harriss, B. 1980. Money and commodities: Monopoly and competition. In *Borrowers and lenders: Rural financial markets and institutions in developing countries*, ed. J. Howell, 107-130. London: Overseas Development Institute.

Hesser, L. F., and G. E. Schuh. 1962. The demand for agricultural mortgage credit. *Journal of Farm Economics* 44 (5): 1583-1588.

Higgins, B. 1959. *Economic development: Principles, problems, and policies*. New York: Norton.

Higuchi, T., and T. Kawamura. 1988. Savings behaviour and debt problems in farm households. In *Farm finance and agricultural development*, 173-200. Tokyo: Agricultural Productivity Organization.

Hossain, M. 1988. *Credit for alleviation of rural poverty: The Grameen Bank in Bangladesh*. Research Report 65. Washington, D.C.: International Food Policy Research Institute in collaboration with the Bangladesh Institute of Development Studies.

Hough, E. M. 1966. *The cooperative movement in India*. London: Oxford University Press.

Houthakker, H. S. 1965. On some determinants of savings in developed and underdeveloped countries. In *Problems in economic development*, ed. E. A. G. Robinson, 212-224. New York: Macmillan.

Hussi, P., and J. C. Abbott. 1973. Agricultural credit: Institutions and performance with particular reference to the Near East. *Monthly Bulletin for Agricultural Economics and Statistics* 22 (12).

_____. 1975. Agricultural credit institutions in Asia and Latin America. *Monthly Bulletin of Agricultural Economics and Statistics* 24 (6): 7-19.

Hyun, K. N., D. W. Adams, and L. T. Hushak. 1979. Rural household savings behavior in South Korea, 1962-1976. *American Journal of Agricultural Economics* 61 (3): 448-454.

Ibru, M. C. O. 1981. Problems of agricultural finance in Nigeria. Paper presented at the Central Bank of Nigeria's seminar on agricultural credit and finance in Nigeria, held at the University of Ibadan.

Ijere, M. O. 1975. The lessons of state credit institutions in developing countries—The Nigerian experience. *Agricultural Administration* 2 (2): 129-145.

Illy, H. F. 1983. How to build in the germs of failure: Credit cooperatives in French Cameroon. In *Rural financial markets in developing countries*, ed. J. D. Von Pischke, D. W. Adams, and G. Donald, 296-301. Baltimore, Md., U.S.A.: Johns Hopkins University Press.

India, Government of. 1928. *Royal commission on agriculture in India: Report.* Calcutta.

_____. 1971. *Agricultural census.* New Delhi: Ministry of Agriculture.

_____. 1977. *Agricultural census.* New Delhi: Ministry of Agriculture.

_____. 1981. *Agricultural census.* New Delhi: Ministry of Agriculture.

International Fund for Agricultural Development. 1983. *Accelerated development in Sub-Saharan Africa: An agenda for action.* Rome: IFAD.

International Monetary Fund. 1983. Interest rate policies in developing countries. Occasional Paper 22. Research Department, Washington, D.C. Mimeo.

Iqbal, F. 1982. *Rural savings, investment, and interest rates in developing countries: Evidence from India.* Santa Monica, Calif., U.S.A.: Rand Corporation.

_____. 1983. The demand for funds by agricultural households: Evidence from rural India. *Journal of Development Studies* 20 (1): 68-86.

Irvine, R. J., and R. F. Emery. 1966. Interest rates as an anti-inflationary instrument in Taiwan. *National Banking Review* 4 (1).

Iyengar, N. S., and S. Indrakant. 1980. Pattern of asset accumulation in rural India. *Indian Journal of Agricultural Economics* 35 (1): 121-129.

Izumida, Y. 1988. Status of government programmed agricultural loans (GPALS) in Japan. In *Farm finance and agricultural development*, 315-332. Tokyo: Agricultural Productivity Organization.

Jha, K. K. 1978. *Agricultural finance in Nepal: An analytical study.* New Delhi: Heritage.

Jodha, N. S. 1974. A study of the cooperative short-term credit movement in selected areas in Gujarat. In *Serving the small farmers*, ed.

G. Hunter and A. F. Bottrall, 59-91. London: Croom Holm and Overseas Development Institute.

————. 1981. Role of credit in farmers' adjustment against risk in arid and semi-arid tropical areas of India. *Economic and Political Weekly* 16 (42-43): 1696-1709.

Johl, S. S., and C. V. Moore. 1970. *Essentials of farm financial management.* New Delhi: Today and Tomorrow's Printers and Publishers.

Johnny, M. 1985. *Informal credit for integrated rural development in Sierra Leone.* Hamburg, Germany: Studien zur Integrierten Ländlichen Entwicklung, Verlag Weltarchiv.

Johnston, B. F., and P. Kilby. 1975. *Agricultural and structural transformation.* Oxford: Oxford University Press.

Jones, T. J. 1971. Agricultural credit institutions. In *Institutions in agricultural development,* ed. M. G. Blase, 168-184. Ames, Iowa, U.S.A.: Iowa State University.

Kahlon, A. S., and K. Singh. 1984. *Managing agricultural finance: Theory and practice.* New Delhi: Allied Publishers.

Kalyankar, S. P., and K. D. Rajmane. 1983. Interlinking of cooperative credit with marketing: An essential measure to reduce cooperative overdues. *Financing Agriculture* 15 (3): 29-30.

Kanvinde, D. J. 1989. Deposit growth in the eighties: Rural-urban and regional perspectives. *State Bank of India Monthly Review* 28 (3): 138-173.

Kato, Y. 1966. Mechanisms for the outflow of funds from agriculture into industry in Japan. *Rural Economic Problems* 3 (2).

————. 1970. Development of long-term agricultural credit. In *Agriculture and economic growth: Japan's experience,* ed. K. Ohkawa, B. F. Johnston, and H. Kaneda, Chap. 13. Princeton, N.J., U.S.A. and Tokyo, Japan: Princeton University Press and Tokyo University Press.

————. 1978. Savings behavior of Japanese farm households: 1959-1975. Department of Agricultural Economics and Rural Sociology, Ohio State University, Columbus, Ohio, U.S.A. Mimeo.

————. 1984. Trends in farm credit in APO member-countries. In *Farm finance and agricultural development.* Tokyo: Agricultural Productivity Organization.

Kato, Y., and Y. Izumida. 1978. Changes in sources and uses of funds in rural Japan with special reference to effects of inflation, 1960-1974. Paper presented to the conference on rural finance research, sponsored by the Agricultural Development Council, the

American Agricultural Economics Association, and Ohio State University, 28 July to 1 August, San Diego, California.

Kelley, A. C., and J. G. Williamson. 1968. Household saving behavior in the developing economies: The Indonesian case. *Economic Development and Cultural Change* 16 (3): 385-403.

Keynes, J. M. 1936. *The general theory of employment, interest, and money.* London: Macmillan.

Kim, M. J. 1973. A study on the savings behavior in Korea: 1953-1972. Working Paper No. 7510. Korean Development Institute, Seoul, Korea. Mimeo.

King, R. 1975. Experience in the administration of cooperative credit and marketing societies in Northern Nigeria. *Agricultural Administration* 2 (3): 195-207.

Korea, Republic of, NACF (National Agricultural Cooperative Federation). Various years. *Annual report.* Seoul.

Krishna, R., and G. S. Raychoudhry. 1980. *Trends in rural saving and private capital formation in India.* World Bank Staff Working Paper No. 382. Washington, D.C.: World Bank.

Kumar, P., P. K. Joshi, and M. A. Murlidharan. 1978. Estimation of demand for credit on marginal farms—A profit function approach. *Indian Journal of Agricultural Economics* 33 (4): 106-114.

Ladman, J. R. 1974. A model of credit applied to the allocation of resources in a case study of a sample of Mexican farms. *Economic Development and Cultural Change* 22 (2): 279-301.

Lahiri, A. K. 1978. Assets structure of Indian rural households. *Indian Economic Review* 13 (2): 143-166.

Lal, P., and U. Nath. 1988. Nepal. In *Farm finance and agricultural development*, 441-450. Tokyo: Agricultural Productivity Organization.

Lee, C. Y. 1983. *A note on agricultural banking system in China.* Rome: Food and Agriculture Organization of the United Nations.

Lee, D. H. 1984. Republic of Korea. In *Farm credit in selected Asian countries*, 90-98. Tokyo: Agricultural Productivity Organization.

Lee, G. H., and H. D. Kyung. 1988. Republic of Korea. In *Farm finance and agricultural development*, 417-426. Tokyo: Agricultural Productivity Organization.

Lee, T. Y., and D. H. Kim. 1976. A study of financial savings activities in Korean agricultural cooperatives: Case studies. National Agricultural Research Institute, Seoul, Republic of Korea. Mimeo.

Lee, T. Y., D. H. Kim, and D. W. Adams. 1977. Savings deposits and credit activities in South Korean agricultural cooperatives: 1961-1975. *Asian Survey* 17 (12): 1182-1194.

Lee, W. F., M. D. Bohlje, and A. G. Nelson. 1980. *Agricultural finance.* Ames, Iowa, U.S.A.: Iowa State University Press.

Leff, N. H., and K. Sato. 1975. A simultaneous equations model of savings in developing countries. *Journal of Political Economy* 83 (6): 1217-1228.

Leibenstein, H. 1957. *Economic backwardness and economic growth.* New York: Wiley.

Lele, U. 1974. The roles of credit and marketing in agricultural development. In *Agricultural policy in developing countries,* ed. N. Islam, 413-441. New York: Macmillan.

———. 1975. *The design of rural development: Lessons from Africa.* Baltimore, Md., U.S.A.: Johns Hopkins University Press for the World Bank.

———. 1989a. *Agricultural growth, domestic policies, the external environment, and assistance to Africa: Lessons of a quarter century.* Managing Agricultural Development in Africa Discussion Paper No. 1. Washington, D.C.: World Bank.

———. 1989b. *Managing agricultural development in Africa: Three articles on lessons from experience.* Managing Agricultural Development in Africa Discussion Paper No. 2. Washington, D.C.: World Bank.

Lele, U., and R. E. Christiansen. 1989. *Markets, marketing boards, and cooperatives in Africa: Issues in adjustments policy.* Managing Agricultural Development in Africa Discussion Paper No. 11. Washington, D.C.: World Bank.

Leon, Y., and P. Rainelli. 1976. Savings of farmers: A cross-sectional analysis. *European Review of Agricultural Economics* (3/4): 501-521.

Lewis, W. A. 1954. Economic development with unlimited supplies of labour. The Manchester School. Mimeo.

Li, C. M. 1961. Economic development. In *Economic development: Analysis and case studies,* ed. A. Pepelasis, L. Mears, and I. Adelman. New York: Harper.

Lins, D. A. 1972. Determinants of net changes in farm real estate debt. *Agricultural Economic Research* 24 (1): 1-8.

Lipton, M. 1976. Agricultural finance and rural credit in poor countries. *World Development* 4 (7): 543-553.

———. 1980. Rural credit, farm finance, and village households. In *Borrowers and lenders: Rural financial markets and institutions in developing countries*, ed. J. Howell, 235-258. London: Overseas Development Institute.

Long, M. F. 1968. Why peasant farmers borrow. *American Journal of Agricultural Economics* 50 (4): 991-1008.

————. 1983. A note on financial theory and economic development. In *Rural financial markets in developing countries*, ed. J. D. Von Pischke, D. W. Adams, and G. Donald, 22-27. Baltimore, Md., U.S.A.: Johns Hopkins University Press.

Machima, P. 1976. *Growth and development of agricultural cooperatives in Thailand.* Bangkok: Cooperative League of Thailand.

Maharajan, K. H. 1981. Small farmer loan repayment performance in Nepal. Economic and Sociology Occasional Paper No. 846. Department of Agricultural Economics and Rural Sociology, Ohio State University, Columbus, Ohio, U.S.A..

Malik, S. J. 1989. The changing source structure and utilization patterns of rural credit in Pakistan. International Food Policy Research Institute, Washington, D.C. Mimeo.

Matsuhiro, M. 1988. Agricultural cooperative banking. In *Farm finance and agricultural development*, 139-154. Tokyo: Agricultural Productivity Organization.

Mauri, A. 1977. A policy to mobilize rural savings in less developed countries. *Savings and Development* 1 (1).

————. 1983. The potential for savings and financial innovation in Africa. *Savings and Development* 7 (4): 319-336.

McKinnon, R. I. 1973. *Money and capital in economic development.* Washington, D.C.: Brookings Institution.

————. 1988. Financial liberalization in retrospect: Interest rate policies in LDCs. In *The state of development economics: Progress and perspectives*, ed. R. Gustav and T. P. Schultz, 386-410. Oxford, U.K.: Basil Blackwell.

Mears, L. 1974. *Rice economy of the Philippines.* Quezon City: University of the Philippines Press.

Mehta, R. C., and D. S. Sidhu. 1971. A study of impact of medium- and long-term loans on short-term credit needs of the Punjab farmers. *Indian Journal of Agricultural Economics* 28 (4): 489-495.

Melichar, E. 1977. Some current aspects of agricultural finance and banking in the United States. *American Journal of Agricultural Economics* 59 (5): 967-972.

Mellor, J. W. 1966. *Economics of agricultural development.* Ithaca, N.Y., U.S.A.: Cornell University Press.

_____. 1976. *The new economics of growth: Strategy for India and the developing world*. Ithaca, N.Y., U.S.A.: Cornell University Press.

Meyer, R. L., and A. Srinivasan. 1987. Policy implications of financial intermediation costs in Bangladesh. Economic and Sociology Occasional Paper No. 1359. Department of Agricultural Economics and Rural Sociology, Ohio State University, Columbus, Ohio, U.S.A.

Meyer, R. L., C. B. Baker, and T. Onchon. 1979. Agricultural credit in Thailand. Department of Agricultural Economics and Rural Sociology, Ohio State University, Columbus, Ohio, U.S.A.

Miksell, R. F., and J. E. Zinser. 1973. The nature of the savings functions in developing countries: A survey of the theoretical and empirical literature. *Journal of Economic Literature* 11 (1): 1-26.

Miller, L. F. 1977. *Agricultural credit and finance in Africa*. New York: Rockefeller Foundation.

Mizoguchi, T. 1973. An econometric comparison of farm households: Economic behavior in Japan, Korea, and Taiwan. *Developing Economies* 11 (3).

Modigliani, F. 1986. Life cycle, individual thrift, and the wealth of nations. *American Economic Review* 76 (3): 297-313.

Mohnan, N. 1986. Multi-cooperatives in rural development: Mulukanoor shows the way. *Indian Cooperative Review* 24 (2): 115-130.

Mooy, A. 1974. Credit needs for small farming, small industries, and handicraft and mobilization of rural savings: Achievements and shortcoming in Indonesia. Economic Commission for Asia and the Far East, Bangkok. Mimeo.

Mujumdar, N. A. 1988. Rapporteur's report on institutional credit—Rural. *Indian Journal of Agricultural Economics* 53 (3): 538-543.

_____. 1990. Financial scenario in the 1990s: Agenda for reform. *Economic and Political Weekly* 25 (14): 731-737.

Murray, W. G. 1961. Farm credit institutions. In *Capital and credit needs in a changing agriculture*, ed. E. L. Baum and E. O. Heady, 195-203. Ames, Iowa, U.S.A.: Iowa State University.

Murthy, K. G., and P. Prameshwar. 1985. Deposit mobilization by central cooperative banks in Andhra Pradesh—A review. *Indian Cooperative Review* 22 (3): 301-308.

Nair, K. R., S. K. Kalia, and T. K. Kasiviswanathan. 1988. India. In *Farm finance and agricultural development*, 393-402. Tokyo: Agricultural Productivity Organization.

154

Naseem, M. 1975. Credit availability and the growth of small farms in the Pakistan Punjab. *Food Research Institute Studies* 14 (1): 65-80.

Nehman, G. I. 1973. Small farmers credit use in a depressed community of São Paulo, Brazil. Ph.D. diss., Ohio State University, Columbus, Ohio, U.S.A.

Nelson, B. N. 1969. *The idea of usury from tribal brotherhood to universal brotherhood.* Chicago: University of Chicago Press.

NENARCA (Near East and North Africa Regional Agricultural Credit Association). 1987. Report on the conference on repayment of agricultural loans, 18-21 October. Mimeo.

Nicholson, F. A. 1960. Report regarding possibility of introducing land and agricultural banks into Madras Presidency 1875. Bombay.

Nicholson, N. K. 1984. Landholding, agricultural modernization, and local institutions in India. *Economic Development and Cultural Change* 32 (3): 569-592.

Niederstucke, K. H. 1974. A socioeconomic evaluation of the smallholder credit scheme, Kericho, Kenya.

Nisbet, C. T. 1969. The relationship between formal and informal credit markets in rural Chile. *Land Economics* 45 (2): 162-173.

_____. 1971. Moneylending in rural areas of Latin America. *American Journal of Economics and Sociology* 30 (1): 71-84.

Noda, T. 1970. Savings of farm households. In *Agriculture and economic growth: Japan's experience,* ed. K. Ohkawa, B. F. Johnston, and H. Kaneda. Princeton, N.J., U.S.A. and Tokyo, Japan: Princeton University Press and University of Tokyo Press.

Norinchukin Bank. 1985. *Rural credit in Japan.* Tokyo.

Nyanin, O. O. 1969. Credit and small farmers in South Korea, 1968-70. M.S. thesis, Ohio State University, Columbus, Ohio, U.S.A.

_____. 1982. Costs of agricultural lending, institutional viability, and lender behavior in Jamaica. Ph.D. diss. Columbus, Ohio, U.S.A.: Ohio State University.

Obibuaku, L. O., and G. D. Hursh. 1974. Farm practice adoption in the eastern states of Nigeria. *Agricultural Administration* 1 (2): 115-123.

Ohio State University. 1987. Rural finance in Niger: A critical appraisal and recommendations for change. Final report. Ohio State University, Columbus, Ohio, U.S.A.

Olin, M. 1975. The distribution of agricultural credit in Latin America. Tel Aviv University, Tel Aviv, Israel. Mimeo.

Olu, W. 1985. *Formal credit and default problems in IRD-Programmes in Sierra Leone.* Hamburg, Germany: Studien zur Integrierten Ländlichen Entwicklung, Verlag Weltarchiv.

Oluwasanmi, H. A., and J. A. Alao. 1965. The role of credit in the transformation of traditional agriculture: The Western Nigerian experience. *The Nigerian Journal of Economics and Social Studies* 7 (1): 31-50.

Onchon, T. 1982. Credit problems of farmers in Thailand. Paper prepared for the symposium on farm credit organized by the Asian Productivity Center, Manila.

————. 1988. Farm credit policies in Asian countries. In *Farm finance and agricultural development*, 343-354. Tokyo: Agricultural Productivity Organization.

Ong, M. M. L. 1972. Changes in farm-level savings and consumption in Taiwan, 1960-1970. Ph.D. diss., Ohio State University, Columbus, Ohio, U.S.A.

Ong, M. M. L., D. W. Adams, and I. J. Singh. 1976. Voluntary rural savings capacities in Taiwan, 1960-1970. *American Journal of Agricultural Economics* 58 (3): 578-582.

Osuntogun, A. 1980. Farm level credit use among cooperative farmers in Nigeria. In *Borrowers and lenders: Rural financial markets and institutions in developing countries*, ed. J. Howell. London: Overseas Development Institute.

Padki, M. B., and G. S. Gajarajan. 1978. Some basic conflicts in rural credit: With special reference to farmers' service cooperative societies. *Indian Journal of Agricultural Economics* 33 (4): 84-91.

Padmanabhan, K. P. 1988. *Rural credit: Lessons for rural bankers and policy makers.* London: Intermediate Technology Publications.

Pakistan, Government of. 1974. *Report on the rural credit survey.* Lahore: Agricultural Census Organization.

Pani, P. K. 1966. Cultivator's demand for credit: A cross-section analysis. *International Economic Review* 7 (2): 176-203.

Paniker, P. G. K. 1970. *Rural saving in India.* Bombay: Somaiya Publications.

Parks, L. L., and R. L. Tinnermeier. 1981. Agricultural credit for farmer groups: Experiments in Honduras. CERCA.

Pathak, S. M., and T. Shukla. 1987a. Performance of the organized rural financial markets in agricultural sector: Some issues. *Prajnan* 16 (4): 491-513.

————. 1987b. Regional variations in flow of funds and functioning of rural financial market. *Prajnan* 16 (4): 477-489.

Patrick, H. T. 1966. Financial development and economic growth in underdeveloped countries. *Economic Development and Cultural Change* 14 (2): 174-189.

Paulson, J. 1984. The structure and development of financial markets in Kenya: An example of agricultural finance. Ph.D. diss., Stanford University, Stanford, Calif., U.S.A.

Penny, D. 1968. Farm credit policy in the early stages of agricultural development. *Australian Journal of Agricultural Economics* 12 (1): 32-45.

Penson, J. B., Jr. 1972. Demand for financial assets in the farm sector: A portfolio balance approach. *American Journal of Agricultural Economics* 54 (2): 163-174.

Peres, F. C. 1976. Derived demand for credit under conditions of risk. Ph.D. diss., Ohio State University, Columbus, Ohio, U.S.A.

Philippines, Republic of. 1978. *A study of the nonrepayment of agricultural loans in the Philippines.* Manila: Presidential Committee on Agricultural Credit, Technical Board for Agricultural Credit.

————. 1979. Effectiveness of financial institutions and cooperatives to mobilize savings R07-70, Circa 1979. Mimeo.

Philippines, Bureau of Cooperatives Development. 1979. *Annual report.* Quezon City, Philippines: Ministry of Local Government and Community Development.

Prabhu, S. K. 1988. Rural credit structure in India: Trends and implications. Paper presented at the National Conference on Banking Development, organized by the Reserve Bank of India, at Bombay.

Prabhu, S. K., A. Nadkarni, and C. V. Achutan. 1988. Rural credit: Mystery of the missing households. Special articles, *Economic and Political Weekly* 23 (50): 2642-2646.

Rahman, A. n.d. Structure and capital accumulation in Bangladesh agriculture: A case of low level equilibrium trap. Mimeo.

Raj, K. N. 1962. The marginal rate of saving in Indian economy. *Oxford Economic Papers* 14 (1): 36-50.

Rajagopalan, V., and S. Krishnamoorthy. 1969. Savings elasticities and strategies for capital formation: A micro analysis. *Indian Journal of Agricultural Economics* 24 (4): 110-116.

Rana, J. M. 1973. *Multipurpose cooperative societies since nationalization.* New Delhi: International Cooperative Alliance, Regional Office and Education Centre for Southeast Asia.

Rangarajan, C. 1974. Banking development since nationalization. *Sankhya, Indian Journal of Statistics* 34 (Series C, Parts 2 and 4): 417-440.

Rao, B. P. 1970. The economics of agricultural credit use in southern Brazil. Ph.D. diss., Ohio State University, Columbus, Ohio, U.S.A.

Rao, K. V., and V. Mohandass. 1986. Cooperative credit: Certain dimensions and problems. *Indian Cooperative Review* 23 (3): 255-268.

Reserve Bank of India. 1945. *Report of the agricultural finance sub-committee.* Bombay.

_____. 1951. *Report of the all-India rural credit survey, 1951/52.* Bombay.

_____. 1954. *All-India rural credit survey: Report of the committee on directions,* vol. I and II. Bombay.

_____. 1969. *Report of the all-India rural credit review committee.* Bombay.

_____. 1992. *A review of agricultural credit in India.* Bombay: Agricultural Credit Review Committee.

_____. Various issues a. *Banking statistical returns.* Bombay.

_____. Various issues b. *Statistical statements relating to cooperative movement in India, part I.* Bombay.

Revell, J. 1980. *Costs and margins in banking: An international survey.* Paris: Organization for Economic Cooperation and Development.

Roongtanapirom, T. 1975. Thai commercial banking of the 1980's. In *Finance, trade and economic development,* ed. P. Sondysuvan: 93-97. Bangkok: Sompong Press.

Rosegrant, M. W., and A. Siamwalla. 1988. Government credit programs: Justification, benefits, and costs. In *Agricultural price policy for developing countries,* ed. J. W. Mellor and R. Ahmed, 219-238. Baltimore, Md., U.S.A.: Johns Hopkins University Press for the International Food Policy Research Institute.

Rosen, G. 1975. *Peasant society in a changing economy: Comparative development in Southeast Asia and India.* Urbana, Ill., U.S.A.: University of Illinois.

Rudra, A. 1978. Saving, investment, and consumption. In *Database of Indian economy: Review and reappraisal,* vol. 1, ed. C. R. Rao. Calcutta and Hyderabad: Statistical Publishing Society and the Indian Econometric Society.

Ruozi, R. 1979. A survey of agricultural credit in the E.E.C. A paper presented at the Second International Conference on Rural Finance Research Issues, 29 August to 1 September, Calgary, Alberta, Canada.

Ruthenberg, H. 1977. The adoption of agricultural production services to changing circumstances. *Agricultural Administration* 4 (2).

Sahani, B. S. 1967. *Saving and economic development.* Calcutta: Scientific Book Agency.

Saito, K. A., and D. P. Villanueva. 1981. Transaction costs of credit to small-scale sector in the Philippines. *Economic Development and Cultural Change* 29 (3): 631-640.

Sanderatne, N. 1970. Agricultural credit: Ceylon's experience. *South Asian Review* 3 (3).

Sarma, P. V., and K. S. Prasad. 1978. Demand for credit in Andhra Pradesh. *Indian Journal of Agricultural Economics* 33 (4): 99-105.

Schaefer-Kehnert, W. 1983. Success with group lending in Malawi. In *Rural financial markets in developing countries,* ed. J. D. Von Pischke, D. W. Adams, and G. Donald, 278-283. Baltimore, Md., U.S.A.: Johns Hopkins University Press.

Schluter, M. G. 1974. *The interaction of credit and uncertainty in determining resource allocation and incomes on small farms, Sural District, India.* Occasional Paper No. 68. Ithaca, N.Y., U.S.A.: Department of Agricultural Economics, Cornell University.

Schultz, T. 1964. *Transforming traditional agriculture.* Chicago: University of Chicago Press.

Schumpeter, J. A. 1934. *The theory of economic development: An inquiry into profits, capital, credit, interest rate, and the business cycle.* Cambridge, Mass., U.S.A.: Harvard University Press.

_____. 1939. *Business cycles: A theoretical, historical, and statistical analysis of the capital process.* 2 vols. New York: McGraw-Hill.

Seetharaman, S. P., and B. M. Desai. 1987. Management education for cooperative personnel in India: Status, problem, and a strategic perspective. Paper presented to the conference on management education in India: Problems and prospects, held at the Indian Institute of Management, Ahmedabad.

Shaw, E. S. 1973. *Financial deepening in economic development.* New York: Oxford University Press.

Shinohara, M. 1968. Savings behavior of the farm households. *The Economic Studies Quarterly* 29 (2).

Shukla, T. 1971. Regional analysis of institutional finance for agriculture. *Indian Journal of Agricultural Economics* 24 (4): 542-554.

_____. 1985. Agricultural overdues: A myth or reality? *The Economic Times* (January 29).

Siamwalla, A., et al. 1989. The Thai rural credit system: A description and elements of a theory. Paper presented at the World Bank conference on agricultural development policies and the theory of rural organization held in Annapolis, Maryland, U.S.A.

159

Singh, G., and S. R. Asokan. 1988. *Institutional finance in rural India: Efficiency and efficacy.* New Delhi: Oxford and IBH.

Singh, I., and C. Y. Ahn. 1978. A dynamic multi-commodity model of the agricultural sector: A regional application in Brazil. *European Economic Review* 11 (2): 155-179.

Singh, M. 1970. *Cooperatives in Asia.* New York: Praeger.

Singh, U. S., and D. Jha. 1971. A normative analysis of the impact of capital availability on farm income and demand for short-term credit on farms in Delhi. *Indian Journal of Agricultural Economics* 26 (4): 524-532.

Snyder, D. W. 1974. Econometric studies of household saving behavior in developing countries: A survey. *The Journal of Development Studies* 10 (2): 139-153.

Srinivasan, A., and R. L. Meyer. 1986. *An empirical analysis of rural deposit mobilization in South Asia.* Economic and Sociology Occasional Paper 1249. Columbus, Ohio, U.S.A.: Ohio State University.

_____. 1988. A multiproduct cost study of rural bank branches in Bangladesh. Ohio State University, Columbus, Ohio, U.S.A.

_____. n.d. The impact of bank branches, rural income, and deposit interest rates on rural deposits in South Asia. Economic and Sociology Occasional Paper 1299. Ohio State University, Columbus, Ohio, U.S.A.

State Bank of India Staff College. 1973. *Report on the Indian/FAO seminar on agricultural banking.* Hyderabad, India.

Stickley, T., and E. Tapsoba. 1980. Loan repayment delinquency in Upper Volta. In *Borrowers and lenders: Rural financial markets and institutions in developing countries,* ed. J. Howell, 273-285. London: Overseas Development Institute.

Stockhausen, J. von. 1983. Guarantee funds and the provision of capital in the self-help sphere. In *Rural financial markets in developing countries,* ed. J. D. Von Pischke, D. W. Adams, and G. Donald. Baltimore, Md., U.S.A.: Johns Hopkins University Press.

Stone, B. 1988. Developments in agricultural technology. *The China Quarterly* (December).

Subido, C. T. 1961. Rural savings behavior. Discussion Paper No. 8111. University of the Philippines, Quezon City, the Philippines.

Sugianto. 1972. Problems of lending institutions: Bank Rakyat Indonesia experience. Paper presented at the symposium on credit held by the Asian Productivity Organization, Tokyo.

Tapsoba, E. K. 1981. An economic and institutional analysis of formal and informal credit in eastern Upper Volta: Empirical evidences and policy implications. Ph.D. diss., Michigan State University, Ann Arbor, Mich., U.S.A.

Tashiro, T. 1984. *An outline of credit activities of agricultural cooperatives.* Tokyo: The Institute for the Development of Agricultural Cooperation in Asia.

Taylor, L. 1979. *Macro models for developing countries.* New York: McGraw-Hill.

————. 1981. IS/LM in the tropics: Diagramatics of the new structuralist macro critique. In *Economic stabilization in developing countries,* ed. W. R. Cline and S. Weintraub, 465-503. Washington, D.C.: Brookings Institution.

————. 1983. *Structuralist macroeconomics: Applicable models for the Third World.* New York: Basic Books.

Thailand, Ministry of Agriculture and Cooperatives, Cooperatives Promotion Department. 1979. *Cooperatives in Thailand.* Bangkok: Ministry of Agriculture and Cooperatives.

Thingalaya, N. K. 1980. *The impact of a new bank branch on household savings and borrowings.* Washington, D.C.: World Bank.

Tinnermeier, R. 1977. Rural financial markets: A critical problem area. *Savings and Development* 1 (3).

Tobin, J. 1965. Money and economic growth. *Econometrica* 33 (4): 671-684.

Tuan, C. 1973. Determinants of financial savings in Taiwanese farmers' associations, 1960 to 1970. Ph.D. diss., Ohio State University, Columbus, Ohio, U.S.A.

Tyagi, A. K., and U. K. Pandey. 1982. A note on the application of profit function in agricultural finance. *Indian Journal of Agricultural Economics* 37 (2): 191-198.

United Nations Secretariat. 1980. *Household saving behavior.* Department of International Economic and Social Affairs, Fiscal and Financial Branch Working Paper No. 10. New York: UN.

Vardachary, T. 1980. Problems involved in the mobilization of savings of inhabitants of rural areas and of low-income groups in India. Paper prepared for the United Nations international symposium on the mobilization of personal savings in developing countries, 4-9 February, Kingston, Jamaica.

Varde, V., and S. P. Singh. 1982. Profitability performance of regional rural banks from 1978 to 1980. *Prajnan* 11 (4): 247-256.

————. 1983. *Profitability of commercial banks.* Bombay: National Institute of Bank Management.

Verghese, S. K. 1983. *Profits and profitability of Indian commercial banks in the seventies.* Bombay: National Institute of Bank Management.

Virmani, A. 1984. *Evaluation of financial policy: Credit allocation in Bangladesh.* World Bank Staff Working Paper No. 672. Washington, D.C.: World Bank.

Vogel, R. C. 1981. Rural financial market performance: Implications of low delinquency rates. *American Journal of Agricultural Economics* 63 (1): 58-65.

Von Pischke, J. D. 1983. The pitfalls of specialized farm credit institutions in low-income countries. In *Rural financial markets in developing countries,* ed. J. D. Von Pischke, D. W. Adams, and G. Donald, 175-182. Baltimore, Md., U.S.A.: Johns Hopkins University Press.

Von Pischke, J. D., and D. W. Adams. 1980. Fungibility and the design and evaluation of agricultural credit projects. *American Journal of Agricultural Economics* 62 (4): 719-726.

Von Pischke, J. D., D. W. Adams, and G. Donald, eds. 1983. *Rural financial markets in developing countries.* Baltimore, Md., U.S.A.: Johns Hopkins University Press.

Wai U. T. 1972. *Financial intermediaries and national savings in developing countries.* New York: Praeger.

————. 1980. A revisit to interest rates outside the organized money markets of underdeveloped countries. In *Money and monetary policy in less developed countries: A survey of issues and evidence,* ed. W. L. Coats, Jr. and D. R. Khatkhate. Oxford: Pergamon Press.

Wattanasiritham, P. 1975. Thailand's financial institutions. In *Finance, trade and economic development in Thailand,* ed. P. Sondysuvan. Bangkok: Sompong Press.

Wells, R. J. G. 1978. An input credit programme for small farmers in West Malaysia. *Journal of Administration Overseas* 17 (1): 4-16.

Wharton, C. R., Jr. 1983. The ACAR program in Minas Gerais, Brazil. In *Rural financial markets in developing countries,* ed. J. D. Von Pischke, D. W. Adams, and G. Donald, 200-205. Baltimore, Md., U.S.A.: Johns Hopkins University Press.

Widayati. 1985. Indonesia. In *Farm finance and agricultural development.* Tokyo: Agricultural Productivity Organization.

Wijnbergen, S. van. 1983a. Credit policy, inflation, and growth in financially repressed economy. *Journal of Development Economics* 13 (1 and 2): 45-65.

162

_____. 1983b. Interest rate management in developing countries: Theory and simulation results for South Korea. Staff Working Paper No. 593. Washington, D.C.: World Bank.

_____. 1983c. Interest rate management in LDCs. *Journal of Monetary Economics* 12 (3): 433-452.

_____. 1983d. Stagflationary effects of monetary stabilization policies: A quantitative analysis of South Korea. *Journal of Development Economics* 10 (2): 133-169.

_____. 1985. Macroeconomic effects of changes in bank interest rates: Simulation results for South Korea. *Journal of Development Economics* 18 (2 and 3): 541-554.

Williamson, J. G. 1968. Personal saving in developing nations: An intertemporal cross-section from Asia. *The Economic Record* 44 (106): 194-210.

_____. 1977. Have Koreans saved too little in the past and will they do so in the future? University of Wisconsin, Madison, Wis., U.S.A. Mimeo.

Wilson, F. A. 1974. The role of commercial banks in financing farmers: Some reflections on the situation in Zambia. *Agricultural Administration* 1 (2): 245-257.

Wiseman, J., and T. Hitiris. 1980. The mobilization of savings in developing countries: A position paper. Paper presented at the international symposium on the mobilization of personal savings in developing countries, sponsored by the United Nations, Kingston, Jamaica, January-February.

World Bank. 1973. *Agricultural credit.* Sector Policy Paper. Washington, D.C.: World Bank.

_____. 1983. *Accelerated development in Sub-Saharan Africa: An agenda for action.* Washington, D.C.: World Bank.

Youngjohns, B. J. 1983. Cooperatives and credit: A reexamination. In *Rural financial markets in developing countries,* ed. J. D. Von Pischke, D. W. Adams, and G. Donald, 346-353. Baltimore, Md., U.S.A.: Johns Hopkins University Press.

Yusuf, S., and R. K. Peters. 1984. *Savings behavior and its implications for domestic resource mobilization: The case of the Republic of Korea.* World Bank Staff Paper No. 628. Washington, D.C.: World Bank.